PREVENTING GOOD PEOPLE FROM DOING BAD THINGS

IMPLEMENTING LEAST PRIVILEGE

John Mutch
Brian Anderson

Apress®

Preventing Good People from Doing Bad Things: Implementing Least Privilege

ISBN-13 (pbk): 978-1-4302-3921-5

ISBN-13 (electronic): 978-1-4302-3922-2

Trademarked names may appear in this book. Rather than use a trademark symbol with every occurrence of a trademarked name, we use the names only in an editorial fashion and to the benefit of the trademark owner, with no intention of infringement of the trademark.

Lead Editor: Jeffrey Pepper
Editorial Board: Steve Anglin, Mark Beckner, Ewan Buckingham, Gary Cornell, Jonathan Gennick, Jonathan Hassell, Michelle Lowman, James Markham, Matthew Moodie, Jeff Olson, Jeffrey Pepper, Frank Pohlmann, Douglas Pundick, Ben Renow-Clarke, Dominic Shakeshaft, Matt Wade, Tom Welsh
Coordinating Editor: Jennifer L. Blackwell
Copy Editor: Ralph Moore
Compositor: Mary Sudul
Indexer: SPi Global
Cover Designer: Anna Ishschenko

Distributed to the book trade worldwide by Springer-Verlag New York, Inc., 233 Spring Street, 6th Floor, New York, NY 10013. Phone 1-800-SPRINGER, fax 201-348-4505, e-mail orders-ny@springer-sbm.com, or visit www.springeronline.com.

For information on translations, please contact us by e-mail at info@apress.com, or visit www.apress.com.

Apress and friends of ED books may be purchased in bulk for academic, corporate, or promotional use. eBook versions and licenses are also available for most titles. For more information, reference our Special Bulk Sales–eBook Licensing web page at www.apress.com/bulk-sales. To place an order, email your request to support@apress.com

With gratitude to the BeyondTrust team and Brian Anderson for his insightful work on this project and with love to my four children Natalie, Garrett, Annabelle, and Lauren, whose support and love sustain me every day.
—John

For all of those "insider heroes" who fight to prevent the misuse of privilege on a daily basis in order to help secure precious information assets.
—Brian

Contents

About the Authors

 **John Mutch** has been an operating executive and investor in the technology industry for over 30 years and has a long, sustained track record of creating shareholder value through both activities. Since 2008, he has served as chief executive officer (CEO) at BeyondTrust, the industry leader in mitigating insider threats across physical, virtual, and cloud information technology. Prior to joining BeyondTrust, Mutch was a founder and managing partner of MV Advisors, LLC, a strategic block investment firm that provides focused investment and strategic guidance to small- and mid-cap technology companies. Prior to founding MV Advisors, Mutch was appointed by a US bankruptcy court to the board of directors of Peregrine Systems in March 2003. He assisted that company in a bankruptcy workout proceeding and was named president and CEO in July 2003. Mutch ran Peregrine Systems, operating the company under an SEC consent decree, restating five years of operating results and successfully restructuring the company, culminating in a sale to Hewlett Packard for $425 million in December 2005. Prior to running Peregrine, Mutch served as president, CEO, and a director of HNC Software, an enterprise analytics software provider. Under his leadership, the company nearly doubled revenue and successfully spun out Retek in an IPO that returned more than $2.5 billion to shareholders. HNC Software was sold to Fair Isaac Corporation in August 2002 for $825 million. Prior to HNC Software, Mutch spent seven years at Microsoft Corporation in a variety of executive sales and marketing positions. He previously served on the boards of Edgar Online (NASDAQ: EDGR), Aspyra (Amex: APY), Overland Storage (NASDAQ: OVRL), and Brio Software.

Mutch currently serves on the board of Adaptec, Inc. (Nasdaq: ADPT) as a director designee of Steel Partners and the board of Agilysys (Nasdaq:

AGYS) as a director designee of Ramius Capital. He holds a Master's in business administration from the University of Chicago and a Bachelor of Science degree from Cornell University, where he serves on the advisory board for the undergraduate school of business.

 **Brian Anderson** brings more than 25 years of global enterprise software and security industry experience to this book. He has a track record for award-winning branding and product launches, as well as inbound and outbound marketing models to low-touch, scalable, measureable, and predictable results. Anderson is a frequent industry spokesperson and a published author. Since 2009, he has served as chief marketing officer at BeyondTrust, where he is responsible for all aspects of corporate brand development, as well as lead and demand generation to increase awareness and interest in all customer and investor segments.

Prior to BeyondTrust, Anderson served as a serially successful CMO for several venture-funded companies and senior executive at publicly traded companies. At Siderean Software, his branding efforts garnered rave reviews and numerous awards. At Avamar Technologies, his leadership resulted in a huge revenue increase and numerous awards. Avamar was subsequently acquired by EMC. Prior to Avamar, Anderson was program director of marketing for IBM Tivoli Security and Storage, after successfully building industry leader Access360's brand and sales pipeline and positioning for a sale to IBM in 2002. Anderson also served as CMO of HNC Software, and for seven years prior to HNC at FileNet Corporation, culminating in his role as vice president of worldwide corporate marketing. He received his Bachelor of Science degree in computer science from the University of New Orleans.

Acknowledgments

The authors would like to first acknowledge and thank all of the customers, analysts, and industry luminaries who contributed their real-world experiences, observations, stories, and words of wisdom: Mark Diodati, Andras Cser, Sally Hudson, Derek Melber, Darren Mar-Elia, Ian Short, Jim Jaeger, Neil McDonald, Jon Oltsik, Ian Glazer, David Nester, Dale Martinson, William Osler, Keith Lee, Ant Allan, John Sorts, Nicolas Debeffe, Mike Martin, Paulo Pina, Isaac Asimov, and Heraclitus.

We would also like to personally thank Kristen Canady, Nick Kettles, Jim Zeirick, and Hugh Burnham for their invaluable assistance in pulling this book together. Finally we would like to thank the Apress team for their incredible support, encouragement, and responsiveness: Jeffrey Pepper, Jennifer Blackwell and Ralph Moore.

Introduction

Billions of dollars have been spent over the last few decades on corporate information technology (IT) security in order to "keep the bad guys out," but it turns out the bigger threat was and always has been found within the network perimeter. The so called "insider threat," the trusted employee, contractor, or partner, that can cost an organization more on a daily and/or per-incident basis than any outside hacker could hope for.

Whether we like it or not, "good people do bad things" intentionally, accidentally, or indirectly.

In my 30 years in the IT industry, I have observed and experienced first-hand the impact of major architectural and platform shifts on enterprise customers; the mainframe to mid-range to desktop shift that occurred in the 70s, 80s, and 90s were just the beginning. The typhoon effect of the Web and the impact of major cost reduction through virtualization continued the drumbeat. Our industry, in which I have been extremely proud to participate, is relentless and the changes that are taking place now, through mobile computing platforms, cloud computing, and the impact of social networking internally and externally to the corporation will continue the march forward.

Each of these successive shifts has been accompanied by two major impacts; first, exponential efficiency gains and dramatic improvements in the cost economics of IT. We have all seen and experienced the benefits; increased productivity of the average worker; increased effectiveness of global enterprises to deliver products, goods, and services to their customers; closed-loop feedback from customers on products, services, and company performance that enable business agility.

Second and more significantly, these shifts have driven a dramatic explosion of customer, product, and market data as well as the creation of information-related assets that have become the cornerstone of a corporation's ability to compete and differentiate. This trend will only accelerate. 90 % of the data that exists today was created within just the last 2 years. If the volume of knowledge at the dawn of the 20th century could fit into a small box, that knowledge today would fill a football stadium 20 times over.

It is a pattern of growth driven by such rapid and relentless trends as the rise of social networks, Internet video, and the Web.

This set of dynamics set the bar for IT infrastructure professionals and create the challenges that we live with every day. The problem has become so big and pervasive that IT professionals have begun to refer to this set of issues with one generalized term: "Big Data." We acknowledge that we are faced with an incredibly complex and challenging conundrum and we are not sure how to deal with it. How do we make this data available for corporate use, but keep it secure at the same time?

Virtually every IT infrastructure professional, the BeyondTrust customer, lives with one underlying nightmare scenario:

What happens if somebody gains uncontrolled access to my IT infrastructure? This infrastructure includes the network, servers, desktops, and databases that house all of my data and information assets. God forbid: how will I protect this in the cloud?

As I meet with CEOs of large corporations, they have one request of our company—keep us out of the Wall Street Journal. Don't let me be the CEO who lost all of my customer's credit card data.

The richness and sensitivity of this information, much of it personal to the consumer, has led to a series of legislative efforts to ensure it is secured. The enactment of Sarbanes–Oxley, PCI-DSS, Basel II, and a host of standards throughout the world have emphasized this importance and indeed actually require our customers to secure their assets.

As IT professionals, we have another issue, our "dirty little secret" that no one likes to discuss openly:

The Most Likely Source of Security Breach Is the Insider Threat

Consider the following data points:

- It is a statistical certainty that your corporate network will be breached
- 71% of all security breaches come from inside the corporation with an insider acting maliciously
- 92% of attacks target servers

This book addresses these issues head–on: the insider threat and how insiders rationalize their behavior, the techniques they use, and most importantly how you can secure them using least privilege technologies. It uses case studies from organizations like yours and mine, the expertise of industry analysts, business and IT managers, as well as compliance auditors to uncover what to look for when trying to mitigate insider threats and the associated costs. We will also share best practices on how not to confuse rank with privilege and how to protect against good people doing bad things. We will also help facilitate securing the "perimeter within," the physical, virtual, and cloud-based computing platforms used daily by your insiders: employees, contractors, and partners.

I hope you enjoy the book and have some fun with it. The problem is growing and getting more complex. At BeyondTrust, we live every day with a focus on how we can prevent these types of attacks from happening.

John Mutch, CEO BeyondTrust

The Only IT Constant Is Change

"The only constant is change, continuing change, inevitable change, that is the dominant factor in society today. No sensible decision can be made any longer without taking into account not only the world as it is, but the world as it will be."

—Isaac Asimov, Author and Professor

Best practices in IT corporate security must acknowledge the intersection of technology, processes, and people. Yet, all too often, the focus falls to the technology and processes, while the people part of the equation is overlooked.

It's not that companies have always failed to recognize best-of-breed security software or developed robust enough policies with which to execute them; it's just that they have often overlooked the weakest link in their implementation: human nature. This is especially true when it comes to privileged accounts on physical and virtual servers, desktops, and cloud environments.

We will cover the implications of the misuse of this privilege extensively in the next chapter, but one thing we need to recognize first is *the elusive nature of human nature and the implications of the only true business constant that everything can, and usually does, change*.

- Why does it seem as if every time one security hole is filled, another shows up?
- Why do some audits (and auditors) allow some practices, technology, and policy, while others don't?
- Why does it seem like most executives suffer from bipolar disorder (e.g., expecting tight security come audit time, but demand relaxed enforcement for greater productivity all other times)?

Internal vs. External Threats

Security policies are the first line of defense to an IT environment. Without them, an enterprise would quickly be at war. Not only would there be battles between the different support organizations, but administrators could also find themselves battling hackers (internally or externally). There would be no politics from misuse of privileges—just a raw desire to change, steal, or accidentally destroy data.

So, another significant change facing organizations globally today is the nature of information security threats. Gone are the days where the only concern was keeping the bad guys outside of your firewalls and external threats were the primary concern. In those days, the IT security spend was driven almost exclusively on how to protect corporate information assets from any form of external threat. That landscape has since changed significantly. Today, surveys show that compliance and business continuity are the primary drivers for IT security spend and the focus has shifted to dealing with the potential for an insider breach. Figure 1-1 demonstrates this trend.

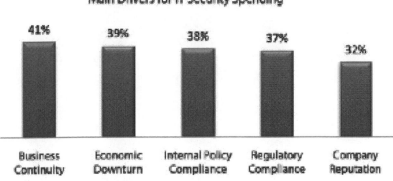

2010 Global State of Information Security Survey
Main Drivers for IT Security Spending

Figure 1-1. Main drivers for IT security spending

Executives often hand off the responsibility for security to systems administrators without providing adequate resources to deploy the authorization controls needed to secure and maintain privileged access. Because of this, a class of solution called privileged Identity Management (PIM) has emerged to extend the identity and access management (IAM) paradigm.

Privileged Identity Management Demystified

US government and private sector information, once unreachable or requiring years of expensive technological or human asset preparation to obtain, can now be accessed, inventoried, lost, or stolen with comparative ease either by accident or by deliberately using sophisticated privileged identity attack tools.

In an effort to improve business security, compliance, and productivity, privilege authorization policies must be redesigned and user permissions more granularly managed. Yet IAM solutions have remained largely unchanged. Traditional solutions account for a significant part of the total cost of IAM, a staggering amount when you consider that these solutions:

- Fail to enable desktop users to effectively do their job as a standard user (80% of employees login with administrator rights).
- Fail to control superuser access to critical servers, giving users complete and unchecked access (98% of all security breaches are committed from servers).

- Force organizations to choose between productivity and security when implementing a PIM solution.

While these challenges may have been historically acceptable, they are no longer good enough in a highly complex and collaborative world, where WikiLeaks shows that anybody's business is everybody's business in seconds.

Here's the first human nature insight—when people think no one is going to catch them, or the lines between what's legal or illegal are sufficiently blurred, many will opt to please themselves first and ignore the consequences until they are forced to. A correlary here is loopholes in tax law— every time someone spots one, it gets abused en masse, until legislators legislate against it.

Specific costs have also been attributed to these abuses that we will cover at length in Chapter 10, but suffice it to say that these costs can range from $120/desktop/year to over $2M per server incident. *These are not trivial costs by any definition for any size organization and could establish this as an area that needs to be addressed immediately, as opposed to an area that should be addressed when time and resources permit.*

It is time for businesses to expect more from their PIM solution in order to improve security, compliance, and overall productivity, which is outlined in Figure 1-2.

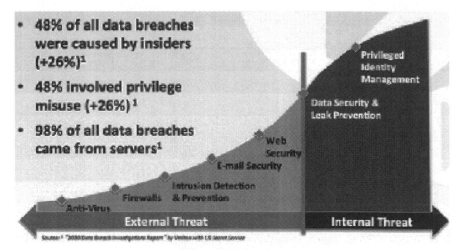

Figure 1-2. Internal vs. external threat causes

Priv·i·leged i·den·ti·ty

Definition: Any type of user or account that holds special or extra permissions within the enterprise's systems; also called a superuser. What is a superuser and why should I care?

Privileged identities are usually categorized into the following types:

1. *Generic/Shared Administrative Accounts:* The non-personal accounts that exist in virtually every device or software application. These accounts hold "superuser" privileges and are often shared among IT staff (i.e., Windows Administrator user, UNIX root user, and Oracle SYS account).
2. *Privileged Personal Accounts:* The powerful accounts that are used by business users and IT personnel. These accounts have a high level of privilege and their use (or misuse) can significantly affect the organization's business (i.e., CFO user, DBA user).
3. *Application Accounts:* The accounts used by applications to access databases and other applications. These accounts typically have broad access to underlying business information in databases.
4. *Emergency Accounts:* Special generic accounts used by the enterprise when elevated privileges are required to fix urgent problems, such as in cases of business continuity or disaster recovery. Access to these accounts frequently requires managerial approval (i.e., fire-call IDs, break-glass users, etc.)

Privileged identities touch upon virtually every commercial sector. This is because every enterprise has a critical component in cyberspace that is accessible by end users, applications, devices, and accounts within this highly complex collaborative ecosystem.

Age of Authorization

Technology is an ever-changing and evolving aspect of modern business. The use of technology is essential to achieving many of the milestones critical to business reform. IAM govern three significant areas when ensuring proper identity security: access, authentication, and authorization.

- *Access* solutions answer the question *"Can I come in?"*
- *Authentication* solutions answer the question *"Are you who you say you are?"*
- *Authorization* solutions answer the question *"What can you do once you are in?"*

Access

Access includes the process of centrally provisioning role-based time-bound credentials for privileged access to IT assets in order to facilitate administrative tasks. Super user privileged access (SUPM) and share account password management (SAPM) are two focal points for proper access controls.

SUPM & SAPM

Industry analysts have classified this space into SUPM and SAPM. When it comes to crashing your enterprise systems, destroying data, deleting or creating accounts, and changing passwords, it's not just malicious hackers you need to worry about. Anyone inside your organization with superuser privileges has the potential to cause similar havoc, either through accidental, intentional, or indirect misuse of privileges.

Superusers may well also have access to confidential information and sensitive personal data they have no business looking at, thus breaching regulatory requirements and risking fines. The trouble is that accounts with superuser privileges, including shared accounts, are necessary: you can't run a corporate IT system without granting some people the privileges to do system-level tasks.

Who Has the Keys to Your Enterprise?

This is where SUPM and SAPM methodologies come into play. So what's the best way to manage personal and shared accounts with superuser privileges in a controlled and auditable manner? That was a key question Research Director Perry Carpenter addressed at the Gartner Information Security Summit 2010. When it comes to best practices for managing personal accounts with superuser privileges, Carpenter recommended creating three types of accounts:

- Personal accounts with full, permanent superuser privileges
- Personal accounts with full (or restricted) temporary superuser privileges
- Personal accounts with limited, temporary superuser privileges

Carpenter stressed that "superuser activity on any of these accounts should be monitored, logged, and reconciled." The first two types are intended for full-time system administrators, and the number of these accounts should be minimized.

"However, there is a balance between having to many of these accounts and too few, and it's important not to make the number too small," Carpenter warned; "otherwise there might not be enough people available at a given time to take required action when it is needed. It's also prudent to consider limiting the scope of the superuser privileges across the organization's infrastructure by asking yourself: Does a given administrator need to be a superuser on all the systems in the organization?"

"The third type of account, the one with limited, temporary superuser privileges, is intended for application developers and database administrators. The superuser privileges of these accounts should be limited to the applications or other areas that they might reasonably need to access." Carpenter recommended using SUPM tools to control these three account types:

- By privilege (e.g., by regulating the commands available)
- By scope (by resources or systems, perhaps)
- By time (either by providing privileges for a fixed period or by time windows)

Carpenter also noted that using SAPM tools allows an organization to control accounts:

- By privilege (e.g., by regulating the commands available)
- By form factors (checksum, license code, IP address)
- By scope (by resources or systems, perhaps)
- By time (either by providing privileges for a fixed period or by time windows)

Authentication

Authentication is the process of determining whether someone or something is, in fact, who or what it is declared to be. In private and public computer networks (including the Internet), authentication is commonly done through the use of logon passwords. Knowledge of the password is assumed to guarantee that the user is authentic.

Each user registers initially (or is registered by someone else), using an assigned or self-declared password. On each subsequent use, the user must know and use the previously declared password. The weakness in this system for transactions that are significant (such as the exchange of money) is that passwords can often be stolen, accidentally revealed, or forgotten. For this reason, Internet business and many other transactions require a more stringent authentication process.

Authorization

Authorization management is a significant pillar in identity security, mainly due to the fact that industries are moving from paper to electronic records. Authorization is the process of giving someone permission to perform certain tasks, or obtain certain information.

More formally, "to authorize" is to define permission policies. For example, human resources staff is normally authorized to access employee records, and this policy is usually formalized as permission brokering rules in a computer system. During operation, the system uses the permission brokering rules to decide whether permission requests from (authenticated) users shall be granted or rejected. Resources include an individual file, task, or item data.

Insider Breaches in the News

We all know that "curiosity killed the cat" warns us not to be too curious, lest that results in problems unforeseen, and yet few know the second half of that phrase, "satisfaction put it back," means that if we were contented, we wouldn't nose around in the first place.

Sadly, that can't be said of three employees at University of Iowa Hospitals and Clinics who were fired after a hospital investigation found they inappropriately breached electronic medical records of Iowa football players; or the four employees who were fired by University Medical Center in Tucson for accessing confidential medical records of victims of the tragic shooting involving Rep. Gabrielle Giffords (D-Ariz).

While neither institution is declaring an official motive, it seems likely it was simple curiosity in both cases. Even when the policy says "don't touch," which in both these institutions it clearly did, people sometimes can't help themselves, especially as when it came to two sets of high-profile patients.

Bottom-line is that while our attention should be on employees with more nefarious purposes, data breaches can also happen when people can't help but take a peep where they shouldn't.

Either way, the solution is the same:

- Businesses don't need to fire employees who otherwise (bar their human tendency to snoop) may be good employees. All they need to do is limit their access, through the implementation of a least privilege management solution. Least privilege is simply granting only the authorization (privilege) to IT resources commensurate with an individual's role and responsibility and not over- or under-authorizing them on those resources.

- As we will reiterate many times, organizations cannot rely on people being competent, or saints, all of the time. We are not perfectly consistent in our principles personally or professionally. Clear boundaries are all that are required for satisfaction to put curiosity firmly back where it belongs.

Reading between the lines in the University of Iowa Hospitals and the Tucson University Medical Center examples cited previously, you can see that even when someone has access, authentication, and authorization, they can still do bad things—human nature is the weakest link in the interface of people, processes, technology, and indeed, *the whims of human nature is the ultimate driver of change as the only constant.*

Privileged Accounts are Pervasive and Problematic

If someone is walking around your organization with a t-shirt that says "Bow before me, for I am root," then you will have a big problem on your hands when the auditors come around or if a hacker decides to target your company for theft or cyber sabotage.

How pervasive are privileged accounts in your organization? Just start with an entitlements audit. Request that your IT department, or outsourced provider, generate a report of every user's access status (i.e., entitlement credentials) across servers, desktops, network devices, virtual servers, and cloud applications. Once you have this, just add up how many times you see "root," "superuser," "administrator," "su," "suid," or any other credential with superuser/administrator-level privileges. If your organization is like most others, you will discover there is at least one account that is shared across IT admins for each server and network device. You may also discover there is one admin to five-ten servers with this level of privilege. If you use MS Windows in the standard configuration, then every desktop user will also have administrator-level access to their desktop or laptop computer. That's correct; every single Windows desktop comes standard with the user set to Administrator level unless someone configures it explicitly upon deployment for the user to be "Standard User" or "Protected Admin."

Now that's pervasive!

How problematic are privileged accounts in your organization? Just ask any hacker what their number-one target is for any attempt at infiltration. The answer will come back as "harvesting admin credentials for direct access to the resource desired." Forbes.com published a story in December, 2010 about two students at the University of Central Missouri who hijacked their way into university computers to not only bump up their GPA but also "tap into the university back accounts and to harvest information about faculty, staff and alumni in order to sell their identities to interested buyers."

So, how do you protect privileged accounts in your organization? The short answer is to eliminate all admin rights across servers, desktops, networks devices, virtual servers, and cloud environments.

People Need Boundaries, Not Walls

Let's face it: organizations cannot simply build walls to protect vital information anymore. However, with the process of adapting to this new virtual collaborative environment comes the enormous challenge of ensuring that privileged access to critical information is not misused. Walls that may have worked a decade ago are now practically irrelevant as users seek ways around, over, or under these obstructions because it interferes with their main job duties. As we move forward in this evolving era, it's important to develop an awareness of how to protect our resources, whatever they may be, using boundaries to guide us, not walls.

Recognize that corporations today are largely information eco-systems; fluid dynamic points of information exchange versus an information silo to be protected like a castle from the middle ages. Then we can observe the "boundaries versus walls" metaphor for what it is:

- *Walls:* Are built to keep things inside or outside of a specific perimeter. In information security terms, that means setting electronic boundaries around IT resources such that only select people may access them.
- *Boundaries:* Are built to guide things along a specific path to ensure proper use of a specific perimeter. In information security terms, that means setting the electronic authorizations such that specific people can do specific things under specific circumstances.

Having well-defined awareness of boundaries enables end users and applications to communicate freely within an IT environment without worry of intentional, accidental, or indirect misuse of privilege. Boundaries allow a more productive and compliant dialogue to take place between users and the IT department and proactively deters attempts of misuse. If boundaries are respected, then IT remains in control of security, compliance, and productivity, and has the authority to take proactive steps by which to protect the enterprise. Figure 1-3 demonstrates this point.

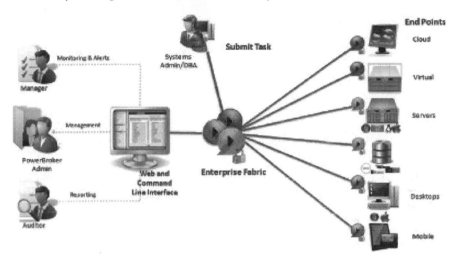

Figure 1-3. Least privilege gives boundaries, not walls.

Top 10 Reasons to Care About Who Has Privileged Access to Your IT

Taking a more tongue-in-cheek approach to highlighting the types of privileged access that occur daily inside most organizations, we thought that a top-ten—list approach might appeal to you as well. How many of these have you seen throughout your organization?

> *#10:* Michelle, the CEO's Exec Admin, won't be able to sell electronic access to company secrets to Julian Assange for his new book deal on WikiLeaks.

> *#9:* Sam, the CSO, can now sleep nights knowing that excess privileges will no longer be responsible for failing a SOX, HIPAA, PCI, DSS, GLBA or FDCC, and FISMA audit (even though he isn't required to even deal with the last two).

#8: Ted in Tech Support won't be able to reset file and directory permissions on any Linux server to which he has admin rights so liberally that anyone with a login can access confidential data just because it makes his job easier.

#7: Sid in Development won't be able to download Apache applications or any other unauthorized open source "tools" that may potentially inject malware into our corporate network.

#6: Fiona, the Admin Assistant, won't damage her PC configuration while trying to upgrade an application by accidentally "fat fingering" the wrong IP address.

#5: Bob, the VP of Marketing, won't crater the nightly backups by loading 120GB of music from his iTunes onto his corporate laptop.

#4: Alice in IT will no longer be responsible for DNS misconfiguration errors, as her role won't facilitate this level of admin privilege.

#3: Fred in IT won't be able to install a trojan on the mission-critical server, bringing it down for four hours and costing the company over $1M in lost transactions, because he was passed over for a big promotion.

#2: Sarah, the CIO, will no longer have to hide Linux root credentials in a sealed envelope in her office safe and deal with a manual check in/check out process.

#1: Tony, the Palo Alto systems administrator, will no longer be able to wear that ratty old T-shirt with the slogan *"Bow before me, for I am root"* any longer.

Federal Mandates for Least Privilege

PIM is critical to business systems, and if not managed correctly, can introduce significant compliance risks. Privileged authorization is critical for smooth ongoing administration of IT assets and if the risk of insider threats wasn't already clear enough, this can exacerbate a potentially risky situation. At the same time, it exposes an organization to security risks, especially insider threats.

On May 16, 2011, the White House revealed language on new legislation directing private industry to improve computer security voluntarily and have those standards reviewed by the Department of Homeland Security (DHS). By increasing and clarifying the penalties for federal and enterprise computer crimes, the administration hopes to temper the perception that the consequences for cyber attacks and data theft are comparatively trivial.

Administration officials admit that they will designate certain privately run computer systems as part of a "critical infrastructure" over which the DHS can have enhanced authority. The agency will also be tasked with working with energy companies, water suppliers, and financial institutions to rank and combat the most serious threats. The new law will also require that these businesses work with independent commercial auditors to assess their plans, and, in the case of financial firms, report those plans to the Security and Exchange Commission. The language also includes the simplification and standardization of the existing 47 state laws regarding national data breach reporting, which require businesses that have suffered an intrusion to notify consumers if the intruder had access to the consumers' personal information.

The result: Many companies will immediately assign added budget and manpower to the task of barricading against external threats—forgetting that these new laws equally mandate the monitoring and auditing of internal compromises.

But in addition to outward-facing barricades, organizations will need to address *internal* access controls, employee IT administrative rights, and user privilege delegation solutions. Administrators should be required to view how data assets are internally accessed (and by whom), monitor changes to application controls that secure and protect the integrity of assets, and even proactively assess the impact of IT changes to business and IT security.

This critical role of IT security is "securing the perimeter within." We strongly counsel that businesses look inward—as well as outward—to strengthen security around data assets by better controlling user database administration and activities and allowing desktop users to operate using the least set of privileges necessary to complete their jobs.

We also can't rely on compliance standards for anything more than setting the minimum bar to establish our security measures; we are back to having to do the difficult trade-off analysis on the real impact of security on productivity versus the benefits. And while there is no simple answer on how to do that analysis, there may be a different way to frame the problem. For example, BGC Partners has adopted a least privilege solution to enforce least privilege security and compliance in their global network, encompassing 6,000 desktops in 20 offices worldwide serving over 1,400 brokers and approximately 2,400 employees.

"Our current environment allows users full administrative privileges on their PCs and we have limited control on what the end user can install and change on a desktop" said Paulo Pina, global desktop services manager BGC Partners. "We have limited awareness of changes being made and in most cases it's too late if a user installs malware and adware, leaving our desktop resources left fire-fighting problems."

"As the Global Desktop Services Manager at BGC, [our least privilege solution], gives me the assurance that my environment is more secure from unwanted software, while also allowing me to proactively control which applications or processes users have access to, without giving them full administrators rights, and the problems that come with allowing such access, yet without hampering their day-to-day job function." Pina added.

Lack of controlled privileged access to critical IT resources carries security risks from the intentional, accidental, or indirect misuse of those privileges, while also making compliance objectives difficult to meet.

Pina said: "[Our least privilege solution] allows changes to be made if required to a system or application policy quite quickly and effortlessly, and most importantly, if we wish, allow us to configure users to run an application in 'logging mode', which will notify us that an application or system process is being used and whether we need to address its privileges."

The Yin and Yang of Security

Sometimes seemingly opposing things actually interact in complementary ways. The Chinese concept of Yin-Yang is used to describe how seemingly contrary forces are interconnected and interdependent in the natural world, and how they give rise to each other in turn. So is there a Yin and Yang of security and productivity? Can you implement security in ways that enhance productivity? We think you can.

- *First, minimize the productivity impact of security by making it as transparent as possible to the end user. Ideally, they won't have to use any extra commands, no pop-ups, no extra screens to go through in order to operate securely. And if the action requested by the user is allowed, just let it happen.* The Windows User Access Control slider provides a great example. If you give users the option, they will turn down the security level to avoid having to respond to an extra prompt. So if you are going to give them the authority to do certain actions after a prompt, why trouble them with the extra steps.

- *Second, while security controls stop people from doing bad things, these same controls can enforce best practice. In addition to controlling actions because of the security risk, we can stop people from doing things that they should not do because of the operational risk presented.* And with properly implemented controls, we can do better than using "Are you really sure you want to" pop-ups that we just click through anyway. Properly designed and implemented controls can enforce a desired way of doing things or best practice.
- *Finally, there is great potential in using data on what people are doing to improve productivity.* Those detailed compliance logs are gold mines of information. You can use them not just to look for patterns that indicate a security threat, but those same patterns can show where security and other procedures such as improper configurations of new systems are hurting productivity. Finding those patterns help uncover opportunities to better train, simplify procedures, and un-cover best practices that not everyone is following. And once those best practices are discovered, you could use controls to ensure that best practices are being followed.

What To Expect Next

The following sections will take a brief look at the remaining chapters in the book and give you a feel for what will be covered in each. The book is in-tended to be read from cover to cover, but each chapter has been written independently for those who prefer to skip around.

Insiders Examined: The Villains

Chapter 2 is dedicated to these unsung heroes of the enterprise. Amongst the usual suspects we will examine include:

- *Disgruntled Dave:* Dave was once a trusted insider with privileged ac-cess to critical IT infrastructure, but circumstances have changed such that he is now unhappy with the status quo to the point where he is intentionally doing harm such as stealing, modifying, or deleting data and/or planting malware.
- *Accident Prone Annie:* Annie is your typical business user who acci-dentally may be misusing her privileges to do things that are against corporate policy (such as downloading software off the Web or

upgrading applications before IT approves) and wreaking havoc on the help desk.
- *Identity Thief Irene:* Irene is the worst of them all; she is an outsider who has hijacked the credentials of an unsuspecting over-privileged insider and uses those credentials to steal, modify, or delete data and/or plant malware.

Insiders Examined: The Heroes

Chapter 3 is dedicated to these unsung heroes of the enterprise. Amongst the usual suspects we will examine include:

- *Secure Sam:* Sam is your typical CSO or IT manager responsible for the governance, compliance, and security of the information assets of your corporation.
- *Least Privilege Lucy:* Lucy is your average network or systems administrator responsible for administrating systems and/or infrastructure, be they physical, virtual, or cloud-based systems.
- *Compliance Carl:* Carl is your classic auditor responsible for regulatory compliance reporting and the auditing of IT policies for enforcement of corporate governance.

IT Infrastructure Requirements Examined

Chapters 4 through 8 are dedicated to examining the unique requirements of physical and virtual platforms, applications, and cloud computing environments. Technology platforms we will examine include:

- *Desktops:* A desktop is not a machine required to be in a fixed location anymore. With technology what it is, that term is synonymous with a person (wherever they may be) that has access and is using Microsoft Windows. People are known to behave differently inside and outside of the office, where the culture is different. Lines between professional and home life become blurred, and people take the suit off at home, log in in their shorts, but that doesn't mean they should take their corporate hat off, as well. But what is the answer? Eliminating administrator rights without allowing for the elevation of certain job-necessary privileges is not the answer. Locking down a system is like asking everyone to raise their hand to go to the bathroom; it shows the downside of mistrusting human nature. Trust is not a value that can be applied in a fixed dose; it has to be measured to meet the needs of the individual's role.

- *Servers:* Servers are the backbone of every corporate computing environment. They are the muscle that maintains mission-critical business transactions, the storage location for all public and private information assets, and the foundation that drives user productivity. They can range from a simple Linux print server all the way through to symmetric multiprocessor-driven UNIX machines executing millions of transactions a minute on terabytes of information. Because of this, they are the single biggest target for insiders and outsiders alike, but it's the insider who knows explicitly where they are and how to access them.

- *Virtual environments:* Protecting virtual environments is a difficult and tedious task. On one hand, privileges in this setting must be granularly managed to ensure complete security. On the other hand, it takes less time and energy to allow users to operate with unmanaged privileges in virtualized datacenter environments. Fortunately, there is an answer to this double-edged question, and it allows for the risks in said environment to be mitigated.

- *Private, public, and hybrid clouds:* Operating in the cloud is the latest trend in the technology world. Whether it's the private, public, or hybrid clouds, it's where we are heading. Just because information and applications are available in such a convenient way does not mean that boundaries should be let down to make all things convenient. The principle of least privilege applies here more than ever before.

- *Applications, databases, and desktop data:* Legacy apps are required for the operation of enterprises everywhere, but the privileges to run them leave gaping security holes in enterprises. The answer, obviously, is not to take away those privileges, but to allow users to run them based on what is required for their jobs. This relieves pressure on IT administrators who think the only way out is to upgrade or pay for an in-house patch. Least privilege truly is the marriage between security and productivity in this instance.

Compliance and Governance Requirements Examined

Chapter 9 is dedicated to examining the governance and regulatory issues ever present in today's enterprise. Specific regulations we will examine include:

- *Government Regulations:* Mandates that require greater privilege authorization control include but are not limited to SOX, HIPAA, GLBA, and PCI DSS. Auditors are well aware of policies that must be in place to comply with federal, state, and industry regulations. Non-compliance can result in fines, severe financial losses, data breaches, and damage to a company's reputation. Sound authorization security will help auditors validate corporate compliance. Proper authorization detection and audit-friendly logs to track privilege use helps an auditor perform the complex duties of this position.

- *Corporate Governance:* Ongoing management of the access, control, monitoring, and remediation of all IT infrastructures is the very definition of good governance. Without a tight and ever-vigilant control on these aspects of policy enforcement, no individual or company could ever hope to satisfy the myriad of diverse regulations imposed on them.

Hard and Soft Costs of Apathy Examined

Chapter 10 is dedicated to examining the methods for quantification and qualification of costs and potential for return. Specific measurements we will examine include:

- *Soft Costs:* To understand the cost of apathy in relation to breaches and least privilege, we must first understand that how we manage risk impacts human behavior. If we box people in by removing all privileges, they will feel suffocated and likely rebel or withhold. If we give too many privileges, people will either feel scared of screwing up and breaking something, or take full advantage of their privileges and abuse the system. The key is to give them what they need; they will feel safe enough to do their job well.

- *Hard Costs:* In addition to the difficult soft costs, you will find a number of very tangible, identifiable, and measurable hard costs associated with the misuse of privilege. Millions of dollars have been assigned to server breaches and hundreds of dollars to desktop breaches. Multiply this by the number of servers and desktops in your environment and you'll uncover a very large financial exposure.

Final Observations and Best Practices Examined

Chapter 11 is dedicated to reviewing final observations and best practices for mitigating insider threats, preventing good people from doing bad things, and securing the perimeter within. Specific thoughts we will examine include:

- *Final Observations:* There are compliance regulations that are intended to protect companies from data breaches. These regulations mandate that security measures be put into place, but many companies, unfortunately, do not meet these standards. Least privilege is the key to helping enterprises becomes compliant based on industry standards.
- *Best Practices:* Thousands of companies have already implemented least privilege solutions across some part of their IT infrastructure and are extending that reach to complete the coverage. By evaluating what has been done by those companies before you, we can uncover best practices to ease the way.

Weighing-In

We will close each chapter by weighing in with our "Insider Heroes." We will use their voice to highlight the specific points you should glean from the specific chapter based on their view of the situation.

Change is the reality every organization must live with on a daily basis and as such, security practices must adapt accordingly. Gone are the days when the "bad guys" were clearly marked as anyone who wasn't an employee, contractor, or trusted partner who could be denied access at the perimeter of your IT infrastructure. Even in Hollywood movies, the bad guys are no longer the ones wearing the black top hat and sporting a cheesy mustache. They look, and in fact are, people you sit across from everyday. In today's security landscape, the focus has shifted from Access (can I come in?) and Authentication (are you who you say you are?) to Authorization (what can you do once you are in?).

Secure Sam:

We just delved deep into ways people and human nature stay the same amid the ever-changing information technology world, and this is a point that is fundamental as we aim to understand ways to offset the consequences of change. People are volatile creatures, and often their expectations are as inconsistent as the net worth of a computer. Businessmen, for example, are a prime example of this. They expect productivity to stay high, and at the same time have zero tolerance of security measures failing. Audits need to be passed, federal mandates must be met, but expenses need to stay low, and the company must remain efficiently running. While these mandates are not individually unrealistic, to expect them all together, without any leeway, historically made daily headaches for any given company's IT department. That was before least privilege was available. With this principle, an enterprise can be secure, stay productive, pass audits, meet mandates, and keep expenses low—all at the same time. Change can be mitigated, both financially and strategically, by giving users the least amount of rights as possible.

Least Privilege Lucy:

It cannot be stressed enough how integral change is to information technology. Perhaps even as central as computers themselves, change is innate in the very nature of the industry. Ideas and practices are constantly shifting and evolving, and this tends to have both positive and negative effects. While technology is advancing and improving, it is also opening enterprises to the growing threat of data breaches. It's difficult to stay on top of this changing environment, and a large part is the number of user accounts requiring admin rights to run. Certain applications need administrative privileges, and those applications are usually necessary for job functions. It's a story heard over and over again; least privilege is the answer. Changes will occur in every single environment, but when organizations allow users to run with only as many rights as are actually required, those changes become manageable.

Compliance Carl:

Indeed, change is the only constant, and as the information technology world around us continues to evolve, adjustments must be made to ensure certain things become a stable baseline in our organizations. The principle of least privilege is one that fundamentally makes sense; it is the gold standard on which we can base all IT governance. Using this concept as the point of reference, it's possible to be consistent in determining what practices, policies, and technologies are acceptable and legal—a consistency that simply isn't achievable without. No longer are auditors able to "play God" with enterprises and the way they manage their sensitive data. By using least privilege as a marker, it streamlines what is acceptable and what is not in the ever-changing world of IT.

Misuse of Privilege Is the New Corporate Landmine

"Organizations continue to struggle with excessive user privilege as it remains the primary attack point for data breaches and unauthorized transactions."

—Mark Diodati, Gartner, Inc.

In organizations, it is a sad and harsh reality that trusted individuals are getting away with too many things. For example, at HSBC, a systems administrator named Falcini had unfettered root access. And what did he do with those credentials? He stole thousands of customer files and then tried to sell them to banks and tax authorities. This is becoming an increasing trend, with more and more breaches coming to light each month.

There are three fundamental misuses of IT privilege that you need to be perpetually on the lookout for:

- *Intentional harm* is the most visible and usually results in significant cost to your corporation. This "insider attack" is the result of an administrator intentionally deleting or stealing data, or planting some malware. To better examine this type of privilege misuse, you will be introduced to "*Disgruntled Dave*," a fictitious character created out of the amalgamation of recently caught and reported insiders responsible for breaches ranging from the obscure to the profane.

- *Accidental harm* is the most common but is usually not measured in direct impact to your corporation. This is the result of someone attempting to do a specific action (for example, install or upgrade software, go to a specific web site, use a system task) and either miss-keys a step or doesn't follow the directions and a problem occurs that requires the Help Desk to step in and fix the mistake. To better examine this type of privilege misuse you will be introduced to "*Annie*," a fictitious character created out of the amalgamation of numerous customer interviews and reported accidental insider breaches.

- *Indirect harm* is the most esoteric but in reality another potential for significant cost to your corporation. This is when some malware hijacks an administrator's credentials and causes damage while impersonating that administrator. To better examine this type of privilege misuse you will be introduced to "Identity Thief Irene" a fictitious character created out of the amalgamation of recently caught and reported hackers responsible for breaches by hijacking an over-privileged insider's credentials for their own use.

Each of these steps is iterative, and the whole process uses feedback mechanisms to continually improve the overall effectiveness and efficiency of the corporation. Let's consider each of these areas and identify the key activities and responsibilities of each one.

Disgruntled Dave Examined Closer

Intentional misuse of privilege often stems from insider attacks. An insider attack is defined as any malicious attack on a corporate system or network where the intruder is someone who has been entrusted with authorized access to the network, and also may have knowledge of the network architecture. See Figure 2-1.

A 2010 CSO Cyber Security Watch Survey published findings that demonstrate the significant risks posed from insider attacks. Cyber criminals now operate undetected within the very "walls" erected to keep hackers out. Technologies include rogue devices plugged into corporate networks, polymorphic malware, and keyloggers that capture credentials and give criminals privileged authorization while evading detection. In 2008, the White House issued the Cyber Security Policy Review, which profiled systemic loss of U.S. economic value from intellectual property and data theft as high as $1 trillion.

The Computer Security Institute and FBI report states that an insider attack costs an average of $2.7 million per attack. CSO magazine cites the following points regarding this threat:

- Organizations tend to employ security-based "wall-and-fortress" approaches to address the threat of cybercrime, but this is not enough to mitigate the risk.
- Risk-based approaches hold potentially greater value than traditional security-based "wall-and-fortress" approaches.
- Organizations should understand how they are viewed by cyber criminals in terms of attack vectors, systems of interest, and process vulnerabilities, so they can better protect themselves from attack.
- Economic hardships spawned by the 2008-2009 recession may generate resentment and financial motivations that

Figure 2-1. Disgruntled Dave.

can drive internal parties or former employees to crime. International consultancy agency, Deloitte, stated the survey conducted by CSO magazine reveals a serious lack of awareness and a degree of complacency on the part of IT organizations, and perhaps security officers. Organizations may focus on unsophisticated attacks from hackers or insiders because they are the noisiest and easiest to detect. Yet, that focus can overlook stealthier attacks that can produce more serious systemic and monetary impacts.

The trial of a former Goldman Sachs programmer accused of stealing source code to take to a competitor began in somewhat of a public spectacle. The Wall Street Journal unveiled some particularly interesting details. For example, the programmer was one of the highest paid in the company with a $400,000 annual salary, but competitor Teza Technologies offered him over $1 million in total pay, including a $700,000 bonus.

So how does the highest-paid programmer of one of the largest investment banks in the world get a nearly three-fold salary hike by a much smaller competitor? We would bet a good chunk of cash that the $1 million paycheck was the price the company was paying for Goldman's code.

Here's the breakdown. He was offered $300,000 in salary, $700,000 in bonus, and $150,000 in profit-sharing. Here's my question to you—which portion of his pay do you think was (could be) the bribe and could the programmer have gotten more? How much is Goldman's source code worth?

We think he was drastically underpaid for the value of the code, but a clean million is plenty to motivate someone to steal data despite the actual value of the stolen property being much higher. Unfortunately, this could be construed as a case of dealing with the symptom instead of the disease. Had a least privilege solution been instituted, he wouldn't have had the ability to misuse privilege and accomplish the theft at any price.

When the trial ended, Sergey Aleynikov was convicted and received a sentence of eight years for stealing proprietary software source code as he was leaving the company in order to sell those assets to the competition for about $1.2M.

The only bright spot for Mr. Aleynikov was that the maximum sentence possible was ten years, so we can only guess that with those other two years, he can figure out even more creative ways to prove insider threats are in fact the most costly.

Employee terminations are, unfortunately, a necessary evil in corporations globally today. In a time of recession, layoffs are more copious and often leave those affected angry and upset. Albeit in a very small minority of cases, some terminated employee backlash has led to disastrous consequences for former employers.

In April 2011, a former network security engineer at Gucci America was indicted on charges that he illegally accessed the company's network and deleted documents shortly after he was fired, costing Gucci nearly $200,000 in damages. Using an account he secretly created while working at the company, the former employee allegedly later accessed Gucci's network and deleted virtual servers, shut down storage areas, and wiped corporate mailboxes.

This case and the many others like it call attention to the importance of having policies and procedures in place to ensure terminated employees no longer have access to company information and resources. E-mail, network, and application accounts must be deactivated swiftly. Employees granted administrative privileges while at the company could also pose an even greater threat. Organizations need to take precautions to ensure departing employees' privileges are revoked, root access passwords changed, and so forth. It sounds simple enough, yet it's surprising how often these necessities are overlooked.

Another solution to consider is looking at the amount of information employees have access to even when they are employed. Are the right limits currently in place? It's much easier to control former employees' ability to access information when they were never able to access the information in the first place.

Accident Prone Annie Examined Closer

Though difficult for many to admit, humans are fallible. We are not perfectly consistent in our personal or professional principles. Accidental misuse of privileges on desktops and servers does happen, and it does have a measurable impact on the organization as a whole. For example, desktop configuration errors cost companies an average of $120/PC, according to an IDC report, "The Relationship between IT Labor Costs and Best Practices for IAM."

Figure 2-2. Accident Prone Annie.

In September 2004, HFC Bank, one of the largest banks In the United Kingdom, sent 2,600 customers an e-mail that, due to an internal operator error, exposed recipients' e-mail addresses to everyone on the list. The problem was compounded when out-of-office messages—containing home and mobile phone numbers—automatically responded to the mailing.

As one famous hacker said, "The weakest link in any network is its people." The most fortified network is still vulnerable if users can be tricked into undermining its security—for example, by giving away passwords or other confidential data over the phone, or performing some activity that allows malware to hijack admin rights on desktops.

For this reason, user education should be one cornerstone of a corporate site security policy, in addition to privilege authorization management. Make users aware of potential social engineering attacks, the risks involved, and how to respond. Furthermore, encourage them to report suspected violations immediately. In this era of phishing and identity theft, security is a responsibility that every employee must share.

A common fear of all CSOs and CIOs is that their organization winds up in the press for some breach of privacy or data theft. So when it happens because of an accident and not an intentional attack, the embarrassment is compounded.

Accidents happen. It's part of the human experience. Unfortunately, there are times when some accidents lead to very serious consequences.

According to a security breach research project done by Data Loss DB in April 2011, nearly one-third of the 25 reported serious data breaches occurred due to accidental employee actions or mistakes, which resulted in the exposure of Social Security, credit card, bank account, and financial account numbers. A data loss of this magnitude is devastating to an organization on many of levels, yet it's understandable due to basic human nature. Companies that don't have preventative safeguards in place can therefore be in real trouble.

Although IT managers and compliance professionals are aware of these potential threats, most are still unsure of how to effectively manage and mitigate the problem. As most network security experts will agree, a multi-tiered approach to threat protection, whether coming from inside or outside the company, is necessary to minimize the risk of data breaches. Unfortunately, not all managers do this.

More Insider Breaches in the News

In August 2010, an Arkansas State University employee mistakenly e-mailed personal information belonging to 2,484 full- and part-time members of the faculty and staff and some former employees. The personal information was stored in a file accessible only by someone with privileged access. Private Information belonging to about 70% of the faculty and staff of Arkansas State University was then sent out.

According to Arkansas Matters, "An employee mistakenly attached a [Privileged] report to a distribution list and that report contained some information about current and former employees, said Associate Vice President of Information Technology Services Mark Hoeting. We're working directly with each of the individuals who received it to validate that the file has been removed, said Hoeting. Even though these steps are being taken, Faculty member Jack Zibluk said they are concerned."

Based on the Ponemon Institute's 2009 Annual Study, "Cost of a Data Breach Report," this accidental misuse of privilege will cost ASU approximately US $149,040. Has your organization performed an IT security review to help minimize any costs associated with accidental misuse of privileges such as this?

Identity Thief Irene Examined Closer

Indirect misuse of privileges is when one or more attack types are launched from a third-party computer that has been taken over remotely. A startling statistic revealed by Gartner in December 2008 is that 67% of all malware detections ever made were detected in 2008. Gartner also estimates managed desktops, or users who run without admin rights, produce on average a $1,237 savings per desktop and reduce the amount of IT labor for technical support by 24%.

The Georgia Tech Information Security Center (GTISC) hosted its annual summit on emerging security threats on October 15, 2010, and published its annual attack forecast report. According to their research, the electronic domain will see greater amounts of malware attacks and various security threats in the coming year.

Data will continue to be the primary motive behind future cybercrime, whether targeting traditional fixed computing or mobile applications. According to security expert George Heron, "It's all about the data," so he expects data to drive cyber-attacks for years to come. This motive is woven through all five emerging threat categories.

Figure 2-2. Identity Thief Irene.

As technology continues to develop and expand, it's an unfortunate reality that sensitive information is becoming decreasingly safe. While this isn't new news (data breaches are becoming as common as a morning bowl of Cheerios), for some reason companies aren't heeding these devastating warning signs. At least Barracuda Networks didn't.

Here's what happened: A hacker, dubbed "fdf," posted screenshots of Barracuda employees, partners, and customer credentials that were obtained through an SQL injection of their web page. Chris Wysopal, CTO at Veracode, offered more information about it, including that, "Barracuda employee password hashes were disclosed to the attackers. It is likely that many of these will be cracked swiftly and that some of these passwords give other access within Barracuda, perhaps through reuse."

Let's take a minute to think about how this happened, or how any security breach happens. The simple answer is that someone who should not have had access to sensitive information did. Honestly ask yourself these questions: if this happened in your organization, would you know whom to question? Do you know everyone who has admin rights? Or whose passwords can grant access to high-level tasks? Do you have a way to monitor who is accessing what and when?

This breach highlights the importance of accountability. In each of our enterprises, we must know who operates with privileged user rights and how their actions can affect the security of sensitive information. Could you answer all of these questions? Or are there holes in the security of your company? Addressing the internal misuse of privilege is no longer a nice-to-have; it's a need-to-have. And if it's not something that's currently a priority in your enterprise, now is the time to make it one.

The truth is, whether it's malware, hackers, or a vulnerability, chances are it's very difficult for anyone to deal serious damage without admin rights. So when we read the latest vulnerability from Adobe, we were eager to jump on the soapbox and scream once more from the hilltops.

Adobe's Shockwave had a vulnerability that could allow hackers to inject malicious code. Now this is where two common but unpractical and unproductive thoughts come to mind on the situation as a knee-jerk reaction:

- *Adobe*: You can blame Adobe for the vulnerability and wait for their patch, but with dozens of common applications that are full of vulnerabilities (some discovered and some not), it's a pretty mediocre (but easy) solution.

- *Hackers*: You can blame hackers who take advantage of the vulnerability for hacking into your desktops (usually after the fact), but just as there will always be software vulnerabilities (and lots of them), there will always be hackers. The real question is: how will you stop them?

It's easy to blame Adobe for having the vulnerability or hackers for using it, but the fact is that no organization should be unable to protect themselves from the combination of these two very likely foes.

If desktop users don't have administrative rights, how much damage could someone like Irene using the vulnerability cause? Any code the hacker injects would most likely install malware or keyloggers, or change system settings such as security configurations, but the desktop would be unable to do any of that.

We all need to stop blaming vulnerabilities and hackers like Irene and start taking responsibility for restricting desktop users so that the users (and anyone else) simply don't have the privileges to cause so much damage.

Even the largest of companies are vulnerable. The headline used by WSJ.com on Mar 8, 2011, was "Google Takes Heat Over App Security" and reported "The company behind the now ubiquitous Android operating system came under fire after computer-security experts last week uncovered more than 50 malicious applications that were uploaded to and distributed from Google's Android Market." In fact, this is not the first time that Google experienced this type of intrusion, as was reported back in October 2010 by the New York Times, A Google employee in China "inadvertently permitted the intruders to gain access to his (or her) personal computer and then to the computers of a critical group of software developers at Google's headquarters in Mountain View, Calif. Ultimately, the intruders were able to gain control of a software repository used by the development team."

But Andrian Kingsley-Hughes over at ZDNet cuts to the heart of the matter in his article of March 2, 2011, by saying "To many of its fans, the openness and freedoms offered by the Android mobile operating systems is one of its main selling points. But that openness comes with a price—it makes it easy for nefarious types to sneak malware into apps. And that's exactly what they are doing."

What Hackers Don't Want You To Know About User Privileges

Believe it or not, there are people out there who aspire to be hackers. Not just the run-of-the-mill, crack a password or two, but a bona fide "Neo" who can play with your secure data like a personal version of "The Matrix."

These would-be data pirates and malcontents have web sites that teach them their craft and even annual conferences like DEFCON to compare tips, tricks, and vulnerabilities. They are more organized than the average business executive or auditor realizes and they are inspired by nothing short of total access to anything and everything on the information super highway, especially what is hidden within your servers and on any one of your user's desktops.

The recurring theme and core principal is basically to find access to admin credentials, and you own the keys to the kingdom. So, when users are granted excessive privileges (admin on desktops, root on servers), then you have an environment just begging for a hacker to attack.

> *Patient to Doctor:* "Doctor, doctor, when I do this it hurts"
> *Doctor to Patient:* "Then don't do it!"

Sage advice that hackers don't want you to know: *if you don't grant admin rights, you don't run the risk of someone stealing them, hijacking them, or even intentionally misusing them from inside.*

Top Five Excuses for Data Breaches and What They Really Mean

In all of our customer interviews and research of actual data breach incidents for this book, we discovered five recurring excuses used to respond to said breach:

- *Data Breach Excuse 1:* It's Too Sensitive to Comment Further, for Fear of Risking Security Further.

  When Vodafone terminated several staff in Australia over a breach in its customer information database that led to a leak of private data, they used this excuse to buy them some time, while they figured out what really happened. According to WCJB.co.uk, "The company said it continues to investigate the matter and is attempting to determine if an employee misused the password or sold it to criminals outside the company. The telecommunications firm said in a statement yesterday that a number of staff had been terminated and the information had been passed on to the NSW Police." All bold positive statements that expertly relay the concern of Vodafone on the errant behavior of one or more of their employees. And yet, likely to be a smokescreen for a company that knows full well what happened, and fears saying more because it was so neglectful on their part that to share the full details would risk incurring serious damage to their very trusted brand.

The bottom line is that it doesn't matter if their errant employee misused the password or sold it to criminals; the employee in question was over-privileged, meaning he or she had access to a server beyond the remit of his or her work role, or, had legitimate but unmonitored access.

Further on, we learn that in fact the CEO has already brought in an independent security firm to review the systems, and to preempt any further leaks, and that the company is changing the database password every 24 hours.

Now if the independent security firm knows their onions from their shallots, they will know that by installing an automated privilege access management system, it would be possible to change the password not just every 24 hours, but every time someone needs to access the server.

A password automatically generated, based on the approval of the employees, requests to access the server, and against the role definition of their job. Indeed, protecting the enterprise from those with the motive and expertise isn't just a matter of mission-critical servers. The mindset that there will be those with access who have IT skills should be incorporated into security in everything we do.

- *Data Breach Excuse 2:* Sadly, It's Not Possible to Trust All People All of the Time.

Amongst many US and UK hospitals and health-care organizations who seem to have experienced data breaches in the last year, Florida Hospital used this excuse when it admitted to a data breach in November 2010. Their CEO was at pains to stress: "While it may be impossible to absolutely prevent an employee from violating our values and policies for personal gain, we are determined to take all necessary steps to review and strengthen our administrative procedures to ensure that we are providing the highest level of data security possible."

We are, of course, happy to point out that with a good privileged access management solution in place—and one that helps healthcare organizations comply fully with HIPAA requirements—they don't have to rely on trust alone.

Accidental, intentional, or indirect, abuse of privileges is mitigated because employees, partners, and third parties only get pre-approved access to the network or servers based on the need their job requires, not their position within the organization hierarchy.

- *Data Breach Excuse 3:* Shut the Door After the Horse Has Bolted.

  This excuse allows the breached organization to sound authoritative by providing an answer to how the breach could have been prevented to the media and public, even if it is a solution they haven't put into practice yet. Unfortunately, the damage is already done and the misuse of privilege has caused significant enough damage to warrant the excuse being used in the first place. By providing an example of best security practice after the event, the US Government took the moral high ground during the WikiLeaks debacle, and diverted attention away from its own complacency.

  Their missive to those responsible for handling classified information, is revealing: *"...create a 'security assessment team' to review the implementation of procedures to safeguard such information, a review to include making sure that no employee has access to information beyond what is necessary to do his or her job effectively."*

- *Data Breach Excuse 4:* Don't Make an Excuse; Blame It on a Third Party.

  Yep, that's what we heard next when data showed up stolen or vandalized. McDonald's adopted the *"we've been hurt too and are in this together"* tone when they warned customers to be on guard against identity theft, phishing, and other scams thanks to a data breach following the theft of customer data held by a third-party contracted by McDonald's. As PC World rightly pointed out in December 2010, the smaller third-party organizations frequently lack the security policies and controls of the larger companies, and provide an Achilles heel that hackers can exploit to gain access to the more valuable network—often flying undetected under the radar.

Our view is similar. With so many potential points of entry to sensitive data and so many different attack surfaces from which infection can happen, a shift in perspective is required. Companies need to think less about building walls and more about establishing clear boundaries. An employee at their desk or on the move, subcontractor, or partner: access to the network should be the same. When we talk about privileged access, it's not who is more privileged than who in terms of their relationship to the company; it simply refers to who gets access to what as defined by their role definition. As the straight lines of traditional security practice get increasingly blurred and permeable, privilege access becomes the cornerstone of not just good network security, but also good people management. Using open source software to solve this problem can be just as bad.

- *Data Breach Excuse 5:* Apologize and Reassure Customers It was an Accident Rather than Intentional Harm.

You guessed it, that's what we heard as the last excuse when data showed up stolen or vandalized. The University of Hawaii used this "cover-our-butts" excuse recently when they realized a former faculty member had inadvertently posted the Social Security numbers, grades, and other personal information of 40,000 former students to an unprotected server. This information has been accessible by a simple Google search for the past year.

"We are troubled (and) determined to notify everyone according to law and committed to do everything possible in the future to prevent this from happening." Their spokesman, Ryan Mielke, also stated that there didn't appear to be misuse of the information. That hardly makes it okay, especially when the information was available to all and sundry for 11 months, and that the former faculty member even had access to the data to conduct their admission research on behalf of the university. Monitoring database access is part of the solution, but addressing the misuse of privilege requires going beyond that. It is just as essential to continually audit privileges to ensure that employees and partners only have access to the minimum amount of sensitive data necessary to perform their duties. This requirement for separation of duties is also a cornerstone of virtually all compliance regulations.

HR and IT—How Security Can Make For Strange Bedfellows

Clearly the best group inside your organization to identity the insiders, and differentiate their levels—employee, contractor, partner, customer is your HR department. This group will have not only their current level of status, but their role and authority levels as well. Because of this, the interface between the IT department and HR must also be solidified in order to avoid the misuse of privilege and prevent the insider breach. Both organizations need to come together to understand that "rank" and "privilege" are two completely separate concepts:

- *Rank:* In most every organization, there is a boss and a subordinate. The bigger the organization, the more layers of management are likely to be found. Ranks define the pecking order or hierarchy of this reporting and decision-making structure.
- *Privilege:* Authorization, or privilege, on the other hand, is about who has access and can do what on a specific system: physical or virtual server or desktop, database, application, or cloud.

All too often, rank is confused with privilege and those higher in the organization are automatically given more IT privilege; usually an excess amount of privilege for their rank because the thought of fine-grained entitlements has not been considered. Fine-grained entitlements are simply calibrating the levels of authorization for a specific computing environment to a specific setting based on policy or role.

The challenge of managing insiders gets a little difficult when migrating to cloud computing. You can control the hiring practices of your own organization, but what about those to whom you are outsourcing? What are the IT employee hiring protocols or security checks employed by your cloud provider? The lack of visibility into the hiring standards and practices for cloud employees and a general lack of transparency into provider processes and procedures, such as how its employees are granted access to physical and virtual assets, make preventing data theft a potential nightmare. Depending on the level of access granted, a malicious outside-insider may be able to harvest your organization's confidential data or even gain control of the entire infrastructure with little or no risk of detection.

But we don't think that security concerns should be an absolute barrier to the adoption of cloud computing technologies. What we *do* think is that organizations are right to consider the implications of the cloud—and demand visibility into their suppliers' technology and processes to ensure the appropriate level of administrative privileges for better information protection.

Perhaps It's Time to "Geek Up" HR

For example, application and privilege controls can provide HR visibility into how businesses and individuals access and manage applications. With HR and IT in concert on privilege user parameters and administrative rights, policy enforcement can become more distributed and effective.

Security is an ongoing, collaborative process. Constant review of both policy and technology is necessary to safeguard corporate networks. And although you can never eliminate risk completely, when you improve relations between HR and IT so that policy and technology go hand in hand, an organization's security becomes a great deal tighter.

Top Ten Reasons Good People Do Bad Things Without Least Privilege

Taking a more tongue-in-cheek approach to highlighting the types of privilege misuse that occurs daily inside most organizations, we thought that a top-ten-list approach might appeal to you as well. How many of these have you seen throughout your organization?

>*#10:* Michelle, the CEO's Exec Admin, leaves her current password list on a yellow sticky note taped to the bottom of her keyboard.

>*#9:* Fred, the Rochester Linux admin, "loaned" his root credentials to another admin because he was late for a dentist appointment and the server needed to be rebooted.

>*#8:* Ted in Tech Support reset file and directory permissions on a mission-critical Linux server to make his data migration project go smoother but, in the process, also gave access to sensitive data to the entire company.

>*#7:* Sid in Development downloaded a couple of neat Apache applications and a few other unauthorized open source "tools," injecting malware into the corporate network.

>*#6 :*Annie the Secretary completely cratered her PC configuration while trying to upgrade an application by accidentally "fat fingering"

the wrong IP address, causing her to lose two days of productivity while IT reimaged her machine.

#5: Bob, the VP of Marketing, now adds 220GB of personal data to the nightly backups as his entire iTunes library of 23,000 songs and 15 movies were put on his corporate laptop.

#4: Alice in IT seems to bring down the entire network backbone every time she has a DNS misconfiguration error that seems to happen more often than not.

#3: Fred in IT installed a Trojan on the mission-critical server, bringing it down for four hours and costing the company over $1M in lost transactions, because he was passed over for a big promotion.

#2: Sarah, the CIO, "hides" all of the Linux root credentials (which are changed weekly) in a sealed envelope in the bottom drawer of her desk and has to deal with a manual check-in/check-out process, but everyone knows where she keeps the list.

#1: A member of the group known as "anonymous" overheard a systems admin bragging over a Palo Alto lunch how no one would ever figure out that his password was "talkingninjamonkey2" after his favorite video game avatar.

Weighing In

It never ceases to amaze us how predictable we are as human beings. Whether it's continuing to repeat our own mistakes or thinking the consequences of others' actions would never apply to us, it seems we're far too eager to turn a blind eye to reality. Reality, however, has a funny way of coming back to haunt us. When it comes to trusting good people not to do bad things, IT Admins and the CSOs and CIOs they report to are like a whole army of Homer Simpsons continuing to stick their finger into the light socket and expecting not to get a jolt.

We have analyzed numerous examples of intentional, accidental, and indirect misuse of privilege and the associated cost of these insider breaches. There are several lessons we can take away from these experiences. The first and foremost is to have an identity management solution in place within your enterprise. Allowing any employee unfettered access to all company assets is both unnecessary and dangerous. The second is to regularly monitor privileges as work roles, new employees, and new data emerge and change. Take the steps now to learn from the past, and prevent any insiders from misusing their privileges on any level. Let's hear from our Insider Heroes:

Secure Sam:

The misuse of privilege is unfortunately a rising trend amid enterprises. There are new data breaches reported daily it seems, and companies and consumers alike are losing faith in information security. Far too many of these breaches come at the hands of insiders. We can't understand why companies don't take measures to protect themselves from these kinds of attacks! The reality is there are far too many "Disgruntled Daves" out there. No matter how large a company is or how much they're worth, no one can afford the risk and the price of a security breach. $2.7 million is a lot of money, and the cost of cleaning up these kinds of messes is only going to rise. So why do companies continue to push the insider threat aside? Maybe It's not just that they're ignoring the obvious; maybe it's that they think that their tried-and-true security methods are still working. The unfortunate truth is that putting up a wall doesn't mitigate the danger anymore—the misuse of privilege is bigger than a firewall. The only way for enterprises and their managing IT personnel to adjust and eliminate these expensive risks is to actually manage access. Companies need to step up and take control of who has access to what, and until this happens, we don't think we'll see relief from the onslaught of breaches.

Least Privilege Lucy:

Privileges are one of the more complicated parts of the IT manager's job. Everyone thinks they need to have power to do everything, but the reality is that most of them don't come close to needing administrator rights, and it's downright dangerous letting them run with them! When users end up with more rights than they need, they inevitably download something with a virus, upgrade software they're not authorized to upgrade, accidentally mess with their settings, and/or just wreak havoc on the fragile network that is so vigilantly managed. Having unnecessary administrators running around really is like a landmine—you just spend time waiting until another time-consuming issue has to be dealt with because someone accidentally hit the download button or upgraded some software without thinking. "Accident Prone Annie" is part of my daily routine, and honestly the bane of my existence. Managing rights is the answer; taking all users to a least privilege model is the way to avoid the ticking time bomb and make enterprises more secure.

Compliance Carl:

There are always issues that come up with information technology. One of the issues that I see all the time is the leaking of that data. Ideally, I see it before an outsider comes in and spreads it across the Internet to the corners of the world, but it's something that's prevalent in IT environments across almost all industries. It's also something we've all seen lately, as data leaks and breaches are becoming more commonplace than ever. What doesn't get reported along with these breaches, however, is the root cause of how they happen. Everyone hears that data was leaked, information was hacked into, and passwords were stolen. But take a minute and ask yourself how that happens in the first place. How can outsiders access these precious enterprise tools? "Identity Thief Irene" is the answer to that question. While she is fictitious, there are thousands of real-life thieves just like her that do the exact same thing: hijack accounts with administrator rights. When a company is properly protected against data theft, hackers cannot gain access because least privilege is in place. By making admin rights something that only those who require them have, information can't be hijacked with as much ease. Least privilege, which is a best practice and a money saver for companies, really is the key.

Business Executives, Technologists, and Auditors Need Least Privilege

"Privileged Identity Management (PIM) is part of the overall identity and access management (IAM) family of technologies, which together provide corporations mechanisms to govern the who, what, where, when and why of secure access management and provisioning."

—Sally Hudson, International Data Corporation

At first glance, one might think that combining least privilege with business executives, IT professionals, and auditors would be impossible given the significant differences in points of view and motivations. Upon closer look, however, this idea makes perfect sense, because it combines security and productivity with rank and privilege.

Indeed, this is not a compromise between the three segmented players, but it makes these forces interdependent and dynamic. In other words, least privilege becomes the force by which each employee is empowered to do what they need to do, when they need to do it. It ensures that they can't abuse their rank, and do what they shouldn't be doing, at a time when the company least expects it.

In Chapter 1, we introduced the concept of these three business roles as "Insider Heroes:"

- *Secure Sam*—Sam is your typical Chief Security Officer (CSO) or IT manager responsible for the governance, compliance, and security of the information assets of your corporation.
- *Least Privilege Lucy*—Lucy is your average network or systems administrator responsible for administrating systems and/or infrastructure, be they physical, virtual, or cloud-based systems.
- *Compliance Carl*—Carl is your classic auditor responsible for regulatory compliance reporting and auditing of IT policies for enforcement of corporate governance.

These insider heroes deal with the harsh realities of rank and privilege on a daily basis as they set about to accomplish their responsibilities within the perimeter of today's extended enterprise. They also have to deal with the differences between rank and privilege, being careful not to collapse these two ideas together.

Remember that we discussed *rank* as the role or position one has inside an organization, while *privilege* is the level of authorization that person has to specific IT resources under specific circumstances. Trusted insiders tend to want to collapse rank and privilege into one concept, which inherently is why good people get triggered to do bad things. Perhaps it's something about the hubris of human nature to assume that the higher the rank we achieve, the more competent and knowledgeable we are. Indeed, this is exactly where complacency can set in—when we achieve a certain rank, we can so often drift into comfort zones that keep us insulated from the need to continuously educate ourselves.

Sam constantly has to deal with everyone demanding administrator access rights (privilege) to specific IT resources, especially their desktops. It always seems that the higher placed the titles and place in the organization chart (rank), the more vigorous the demand. What's interesting about Sam's dilemma is that the requestor usually doesn't know why they are asking for admin rights. They just believe that since their title is what it is, they should have omnipotent access to said resource, in spite of the fact that they might not be competent to do so.

Lucy has to manage the variety of privileges required to deal with IT issues across such a diverse set of platforms as Windows desktops, physical servers (at least four different operating systems and every permutation of version and patch), virtual servers (at least three operating systems and every permutation of Hypervisor manager), infrastructure (at least four different databases, hundreds of legacy applications, and potentially thousands to hundreds of thousands of desktop data requirements), and of course the new rage of cloud migration (public, private, and hybrid). Her persona requires a fluid level of privilege tied to specific policy and circumstance despite her fixed role (rank) in the enterprise.

Carl is a unique persona. He usually sees the world in black and white. For Carl, access to IT resources (privilege) is to be measured against his interpretation of the germane regulations and therefore will interrogate entitlement reports (rank) accordingly in order to determine compliance or the need for remediation.

Let's explore each of these insider heroes in more depth using examples from the global news and your peer community, to further illustrate how confusing rank and privilege can cause Good People to do Bad Things.

Secure Sam Examined Closer

Ever see how a duck glides through water? It looks effortless from the surface, but beneath the waterline is a different story. In reality, the poor duck is paddling his webbed feet feverishly in order to move about. Now you know what it's like to be a CSO, or IT manager responsible for information security, managing today's enterprise security requirements. One of these, or some variation thereof, is ultimately the title Secure Sam holds in your organization. Now you know what his day is like.

At face value, the successful Secure Sam (Figure 3-1) projects an air of calm, cool, and collected control over the enterprise governance, risk, and compliance mitigation requirements. Behind the scenes, he is a whirling dervish of politician meets technician meets mind reader meets soothsayer all served up with one great big stress sandwich.

The successful Secure Sam understands the need for:

- Constant diligence against insider threats as well as attack from outsiders
- Relentless education on new technologies and techniques to control access to all information assets
- Ever-present knowledge of industry and competitive breaches published in the press and on the Internet
- Real-time change control for corporate policy enforcement at every IT endpoint
- On-demand entitlement and audit capabilities for when the CEO, CFO, or auditor asks for specific reports
- A vision of what is possible in his role, when all of the above are competently handled.

Figure 3-1. Secure Sam

The common pitfalls a Secure Sam faces can include:

- Focuses only on outsider threats and over-spend budgets on perimeter security
- Relies solely on trust and written corporate policies for employee use of information technology resources
- Assumes that HR is for hiring and firing, and has little to offer him in terms of insight about how to manage his network
- Remains blissfully ignorant of the impact felt by peer companies and competitors when insiders attack
- Secretly likes the adrenaline rush of fighting outsiders, to the point he hasn't yet recognized the internal threat
- Uses policy changes as job security because his team is the only one with the knowledge of what needs to be done
- Takes two to four weeks for custom reporting when requested

Secure Sam in the News

How much press will we have to endure on the significant problems created by WikiLeaks and the public lynching of those who perpetrate these leaks before we realize that if you give someone an inch (excessive admin rights), they will take a mile (misuse that privilege)?

To use a metaphor: If I sneeze, will you give me a tissue and send me on my way? Will you give me cold medicine? How about allergy medicine? Without knowing the cause, the *disease*, then reacting to the sneeze, the *symptom*, will ultimately result in a response that may be over-kill or under-kill.

Some journalists do get it. Mike Martin at TechNewsWorld published an insightful story titled WikiLeaks Wrangling May Be Escalating Into Cyber-war. He rightly points out "the WikiLeaks controversy could be devolving into a wiki-war."

So why is it that every journalist seems to be focused on the symptom, the *leak*, instead of the disease, the "intentional misuse of privilege" caused by "excess admin rights?"

An article posted on eWeek.com on January 6, 2011 proclaimed "Now, another train is coming and I'm telling you right now, it's headed in your direction. WikiLeaks has brought new meaning to the concept of insider threat by providing a convenient vehicle to empower staff to quickly and instantly hand over privileged information.

Acknowledging the WikiLeaks phenomenon, the important lesson is: your company could be next. Given the volume of leaks WikiLeaks has on private companies, if you work for a Global 2000 corporation, there's a good chance WikiLeaks already has some dirt."

Why Sam Should Know Your Business Partner Might Be Your Weakest Link

The drive for greater company-wide efficiencies and overall cost savings has made the reality of outsourcing a significant part of 21st century business practices. But as Secure Sam has come to learn the hard way, by handing over your data and network access to third parties, no matter how trustworthy, your enterprise could be at risk of suffering a serious and damaging data leak.

According to a new study from the Ponemon Institute, 39 percent of data breaches involve third-party outsourcers. Many companies experienced this problem first-hand when a recent, very highly publicized data breach by e-mail marketing service provider, Epsilon, affected some of the nation's largest banks, and technology and retail brands. This specific breach only involved the release of names and e-mail addresses. However, exposure of more confidential information, traced back to outside vendors, is occurring on a much more alarmingly frequent basis.

The lesson we can all learn here is that companies not only have to monitor their own security, but also that of their associates and vendors. While it is important to provide the information and access necessary for third-party resources to do their jobs, at the same time it's irresponsible to allow vendors free reign over sensitive data or network assets. An all-or-nothing approach to granting users access doesn't work here. Effective PIM coupled with comprehensive knowledge of your partners' and vendors' security policies and practices are the best way to safeguard your company's most valued asset.

Sam Must Arbitrate Tablets at the Office as Friend or Foe

A decision that Secure Sam has to weigh in on now that he wouldn't have had to deal with just two or three years ago is the proliferation of personal tablets and mobile computing devices.

According to Gartner, worldwide media tablet spending is projected to reach $29.4 billion in 2011, up from $9.6 billion in 2010. Gartner also predicts that by 2013, 80 percent of the workforce will be using tablet devices. Whether employees are being issued tablets by their employers, or bringing in their personal devices, embracing tablet computers is very attractive for many enterprises looking to keep their employees connected, while reducing costs.

But mobile malware threats are on the rise. According to Andrew Hickey at CRN in February 2011, "mobile device platforms have become the latest and greatest attack point as mobile device security threats rose to new heights in 2010's fourth quarter and will continue in 2011..." The May 2011 detection of a Mac OS "crime kit" could also heavily impact iPad users and serves as an indicator of what we can potentially see in the future as tablet adoption continues to grow. Presently, most tablet end points are relatively unsecured, which is cause for concern as these devices connect to the corporate network. Data storage on untrusted end points must therefore be heavily weighed and controlled. There should always be a preference for enterprise data to remain on corporate assets, with remote access capabilities limited to secure, encrypted VPN connections, else the potential for misuse of privilege will occur.

Adopting smartphone security best practices will help alleviate some of the headaches associated with tablets in your network environment. It's also important to employ stringent access controls and make sure your end users only have access to what they need to in order to do their jobs.

Least Privilege Lucy Examined Closer

Depending on the size of your company, Lucy (Figure 3-2) could be 1 "jack of all trades" or 1 of 100 specialists each focused on a specific operating system, platform, geography, or business unit. The unifying characteristics include one part technical wizard, one part fire fighter, one part customer service representative, one part project manager, and one part CSI forensic analyst.

Least Privilege Lucy is the first person called whenever something technical needs to be done, from deploying a new desktop, physical server, virtual server, or application in the cloud, to upgrading software versions and patches, to rebuilding damaged systems courtesy of the latest malware attack or user "accidentally" doing something inappropriate. And let's not forget that the CEO will also call her instead of picking up an instruction manual every time he hits the wrong key on his BlackBerry.

The successful Least Privilege Lucy understands the need for:

Figure 3-2. Least Privilege Lucy

- Policy creation; monitoring and management of each role in the organization to ensure against over-privileged" or under-privileged users
- Real-time brokering of appropriate privileges across platforms based on those polices
- Tight integration with existing trusted repositories for policy and credential management (such as MS Active Directory, Group Policy, Oracle database, and so forth)
- A single privilege identity footprint for desktop, physical, and virtual servers and cloud deployment that can adapt to situations based on policies evoked
- Real-time logging for remediation and reporting

- Insight into what she would do with the cost savings created from not having to fight fires caused by over- or under-privileged users jamming her phone line all day

The common pitfalls or traits a Least Privilege Lucy might enable:

- A one-size-fits-all approach to user authorization levels across all platforms accordingly (that is, all desktops use policy one, while all virtual servers use policy two)
- Require only managers or help desk personal to have admin rights to be invoked personally (that is, walk over and type in a password) for every request for elevated permissions
- Assume they can keep up with the level of change required to meet corporate governance and regulatory changes through manual programming
- Remain blissfully ignorant of the impact felt by peer companies and competitors when insiders attack
- Use personal technical expertise as job security because her team is the only one with the knowledge of what needs to be done
- Addiction to fighting fires, because it gives her a sense of importance and allows her to be visible in the organization
- Taking 2-4 weeks for every request not made by a senior executive who will usually get a response within 24 hours

Least Privilege Lucy Is Disgruntled Dave Before He Became Disgruntled

If you haven't figured it out yet, yes, Least Privilege Lucy is actually the same persona as Disgruntled Dave introduced earlier, but with a significant difference. Dave has had something that upset him to the point where he has decided to use his technical expertise to intentionally misuse his privilege and perpetrate damage (electronically or financially), while Lucy still adheres to the values of only doing right by the company. Another aspect of that difference is intent and action:

- *Intent*—Lucy's intent is to use authorizations and privileges as befit the resource or situation, while Dave's intent is to misuse his privilege to intentionally steal, modify, or delete data or plant malware that will activate at some time after he leaves.

- *Action*—Lucy's actions establish a pattern of doing what is necessary in a given situation, while Dave's actions exhibit a covert behavior that may even go unrecognized until the damage is done and he is already in a non-extradition country sipping on a daiquiri and spending the $100 million he made selling your customer files to the competition.

When Lucy Was In Fact David Not Dave

In the press, you will find mostly articles about the Disgruntled Dave persona versus Least Privileged Lucy because most news that attracts viewers is of the doom, gloom, and tragedy perspective. So looking at a case study, we find a great example in David Nester at M.D. Anderson. When David came on board as the Unix security architect at M.D. Anderson, he was charged with developing Unix and web security for the institution's massive information network. Of particular importance for Nester were access control, authorization, root delegation, and auditing capabilities of the network. "The previous Unix environment was not centralized, and it was difficult to understand what activities were being performed at each machine," says Nester. "I was assigned the challenge of placing controls back in to the hands of our system administrators."

David knew that a strong IT infrastructure was vital to supporting the patient care services and overall mission of the institution. "The ability of our systems to operate effectively can substantially affect the critical medical care provided here at M.D. Anderson," says Nester. "If something were to go wrong, we would not have the luxury of time because people's lives are at stake." So you will find that David is much more of a Least Privilege Lucy (in male form) then he is a Disgruntled Dave.

Lucy's Worst Nightmare: "Your Password Is What?"

Who's on first? What's on second? I don't know's on third, and your password is Password? HUH?!? Yep, it seems like the classic Abbott and Costello baseball sketch is now Least Privilege Lucy's worst nightmare when it comes to password management. According to a recent Wall Street Journal article on The Top 50 Gawker Media Passwords, the average user seems to either have a relaxed sense of security, a love for Abbott and Costello-like humor, or are just lazy when it comes to identity-related security. It's no wonder the average hacker can break into sites with relative ease.

Now translate that into what happens across your enterprise when just one employee uses this protocol for personal passwords on corporate resources, which may contain proprietary and/or confidential information worth stealing, selling, or vandalizing. Scared yet? You should be!

Just implementing password protocols is not enough in today's ever-changing environment. The real solution should involve the elimination of users owning their own passwords and implement an automated password management solution. This allows users to "pull credentials" when required from a centralized policy-managed repository, instead of relying on individual credentials being "pushed" by the user.

These solutions create, manage, and remove random machine-generated passwords. These passwords are then transparently used by the requesting resource without the user ever knowing the password or login credential. Therefore, the likelihood of someone misplacing, loaning out, or hacking a password is greatly diminished.

Lucy Knows that Sharing Isn't Always Caring

In kindergarten, we all learned an important lesson: how to share. Some people, as they grew up, seem to have taken this concept a little too far, with no real consideration for possible consequences. I'm not trying to undermine the importance of sharing as a general rule, but let's just take a quick look at how sharing has "helped" in the recent past.

Vodafone. We've talked about it before, but it's the perfect example of how sharing isn't always the way to go. They experienced a breach in early 2011 that affected private customer data. This information was leaked as a result of the misuse of a password. More than likely, the damage that password caused was a result of it being sold or given to someone else. The consequences of this breach were severe: fines to be paid, fired employees, and a whole unnecessary mess to be cleaned up. All because someone was loose with their password.

Every user in every organization must have their own unique credentials. Every time. Sure, it can be easier to let someone use your password. Yes, they would probably end up with privileged access if they had called the help desk anyway. But at what cost does sharing become acceptable? Organizations need not risk sensitive information for laziness.

Companies also need to have the ability to track and log the use of those passwords. Granular details about when someone logged in, the keystrokes they performed, and the information they accessed is the key to correct governance, as well as fast response time if a breach were to occur. Without a system in place to ensure the proper people are using their passwords appropriately, all of your efforts will have been for naught.

We think it's safe to say that sharing is not always a benefit. Should we take it too far and stop teaching children to share? No. Should we stop teaching adults with the keys to their enterprises' kingdom to share? Absolutely.

Compliance Carl Examined Closer

This persona is about dualities: part technical analyst, part financial analyst. At his best, Carl is part Sherlock Holmes and part Judge Judy. At his worst, he is part Homer Simpson and part Harvey Two-Face.

Most business and IT executives alike tremble when Compliance Carl (Figure 3-3) comes around because they know their practices and systems will be scrutinized. Part of this generalized fear is the black and white nature of a compliance audit. At the end, they will either pass or fail. A failing mark can mean anything from small policy changes required to massive financial fines. Because these decisions are almost solely at the discretion of the type of Compliance Carl you have in your organization, the difference between the "Holmes/Judy" version can be dramatically different than the "Simpson/Two-face" version.

Figure 3-3. Compliance Carl

The successful Compliance Carl understands the need for:

- Accreditation with certifications such as Certified Information Systems Auditor (CISA) or Certified Information Systems Security Professional (CISSP)
- Ongoing education on best practices for information technology audit from such organizations as ISACA

- An objective point of view relying on quantitative and qualify-able data directly measured to governance or regulatory standards
- Thorough documentation on entitlements (that is, user authorizations) across all platforms physical, virtual, and cloud
- Ongoing education and refreshers on regulatory mandates and how they relate to your industry or organization.

The common pitfalls a Compliance Carl faces can include:

- A strong IT background doesn't necessarily make for a strong IT auditor as the disciplines are completely different without proper training and accreditation
- Assuming that compliance is a project and not a process that requires ongoing diligence for meeting governance and regulatory requirements
- Believing that once a regulation is published, it will not change and failing to implement any form of regulatory change communication alerting system
- Using subjectivity and personal bias or high-level trend data instead of detailed reports to determine compliance
- Being overwhelmed by techno-jargon to the point of being misled from compliance risks
- Acting like Harvey Two-Face in Batman, using a coin-flip for every decision made

Compliance Carl in the News

What is sweet revenge to the business and IT executive is when they read about the IT auditor who fell under the scrutiny of the press and questions of favoritism arise. In June 2010, CBS News Canada reported that an "Alberta IT Auditor Appeared In YouTube Promo." It went on to report that "Patrick Dunnigan, an information technology auditor, is shown in the info-mercial extolling the virtues of software from New York City company Application Security Incorporated (ASI) purchased by the Alberta auditor general last year. Dunnigan helped choose the software for the office."

The article went on to say "Both the company and the auditor general's office say Dunnigan was not paid to take part in the video nor was the software purchase price reduced in return for his appearance. However, assistant auditor general Ed Ryan said the promotion was not authorized by anyone in the office and an investigation is now underway to determine if Dunnigan broke the code of conduct." Here is an example where a Compliance Carl came under scrutiny for ethics and casts a shadow of doubt on credibility.

This is a real-life example of why Carl is the most tenuous character here. His capacity to hit the common pitfalls and be another "good person doing a bad thing" or the errant ability to confuse rank and privilege will lead him to underestimate insider threats relative to external threats as the weakest link.

Compliance Carl in the Blogosphere

If you frequent the blogosphere on the Internet, then you can also find lots of opinions on IT auditors: the good, the bad, and the ugly. One of the favorite passages we found was on theitauditor.com who, in June 2010, wrote:

> "Another place where blame lies is with audit managers who are more concerned with maintaining the contract than providing the client with the ability to decide which issues are significant enough to worry about. It is my belief that all weaknesses found during an audit should be communicated to the client in writing in some form. I am not promoting the idea that all findings should make it into the final report, or even that all findings are reportable. I am saying that in daily interactions, status meetings or briefings the client should be presented a list of every single finding that was observed, this provides legal/regulatory coverage for the auditors, and it allows the client to make the decision to address or ignore each issue individually. The way I see it, my integrity as a professional is more important than the contract that I am working under. If my client is intimidated by a long list of findings, they can either keep me around to help them correct the situation or they can continue to bury their head in the sand and either terminate my contract or I may refuse to return upon the end of that contract. Auditors are a resource that should be used to help; if we are seen as adversaries to the system admins or management our work will not add any value to their processes."

Why McAfee Knows that Carl Still Looks Outside the Perimeter Instead of Within

To add fuel to Compliance Carl's list of daily action items, you may have already seen the results of a 1,000+-person survey conducted recently by McAfee and wrapped up in a crisp report. They estimate that businesses lost more than $1 trillion in 2008 as a result of data leaks. With the help of SAIC and international research firm Vanson Bourne, the company has added some meaty authority to what would otherwise be seen as a vendor-biased report.

According to the report, the most popular methods of protecting sensitive data are anti-virus, firewalls, and intrusion detection/prevention systems, which are implemented by more than four in five organizations, perhaps followed by deep packet inspections, which was reported by two-thirds of respondents. It figures that all of these are outward-facing security mechanisms primarily intended to prevent malicious hackers, viruses, and worms. Therein lies the problem.

Surveys from the Computer Security Institute (CSI)/FBI research team also show that most organizations believe the majority of their security risks are from external threats, yet actual analysis of real breaches shows that internal threats outweigh external ones. AT the 2011 RSA show we remember one of our execs was telling a reporter that people are finally realizing that their risks are from within. This was also a big story during the recession, where many organizations were bracing themselves for massive layoffs that were creating armies of angry, unemployed, ex-employees. Before the recession, reports like those from the CSI were trying to change our minds to realize where our focus should be—demonstrating the internal problem. Therein lies the value of a least privilege solution to help prevent good people (insiders) from doing bad things (steal or harm data).

And yet, after all that, the industry hasn't caught on. What else could anyone possibly do to erase this perspective that the vast majority of risk comes from over-glorified hackers?

Why Carl Just Doesn't Always Realize the Outside Is Also the Inside on the Outside for Today's Mobile Workers

An auditor's nightmare is trying to keep track of remote users and how to keep track of their potential or capacity for generating compliance or governance issues. According to a Runzheimer survey released in April 2011,

45 percent of today's workforce is mobile. For companies, having such an extensive number of remote employees can provide a number of great advantages, but it has plenty of downsides, too.

Among the top concerns of enterprise executives is being able to effectively manage the mobile workforce to ensure maximum productivity and control the distribution of data. IT managers have indicated that it is a lot more challenging to keep remote employees informed of security policies and initiatives. On top of that, mobile workers are significantly more likely to access dangerous content than those in the office. Additionally, when employees bring their own personal mobile devices into the office network fray, security management can seem like a nightmare.

But it's not all bad. By combining the deployment of up-to-date security solutions with instituting best practices and compliance standards, organizations have a golden opportunity to capitalize on all of the positive aspects of a mobile workforce, while minimizing the potential for data losses, breaches, or even worse. Part of companies' mobile security strategy should also include implementing a least privilege solution, ensuring that remote workers can only access the data and perform the computing functions needed to do their jobs. *Employees can't lose what they can't access.*

So, now we have a better idea of the role least privilege can play in the lives of the business manager, represented by Sam, the IT admin, represented by Lucy, and the compliance auditor, represented by Carl. We've illustrated how it represents a common thread between their roles despite their rank. Let's now return to our overarching concern in this book—the vagaries of human nature—and uncover other areas where this problem occurs.

The Problem Still Exists Between the Keyboard and Chair

There Is No Patch For Stupidity. No, we're not talking about a Boy or Girl Scout patch (or merit badge) now awarded for making dumb errors with information technology at work. We're referring to the ever-present vendor tech support cry of "just install the patch" whenever something goes wrong.

In this case, the patch is a "fix" for the buggy software that invariably caused some loss of data and/or productivity. But what happens when the error is human error? Unfortunately, there are no "patches" for that, unless you count getting rid of said employee and replacing him with someone smarter.

A common cry of helps desk personnel worldwide is PEBKAC! If you don't know what that means, you're not alone. We had to look up that acronym as well to discover it meant "Problem Exists Between Keyboard and Chair."

Accidents happen, and if you are still providing excessive privileges to your desktop/laptop users or server/network/database/cloud/virtual administrators, then you are at risk of the accidental misuse of privilege. Sometimes, these accidents can cause harm that is newsworthy. In this instance, you not only have to deal with the problems created, but also the public fallout that follows from the press and blogosphere.

First, you need to eliminate admin rights on Windows desktops and root privileges off of servers, then you implement a PIM solution to create a least privilege environment such that no one will have enough permission to cause harm if they misuse their privileges. In this way, you can mitigate the severity of potential user stupidity and not have to deal with the help desk crying PEBKAC or fear an unpleasant expose in the Wall Street Journal, local paper, wikileaks.com, or the blogosphere.

The Swiss Cheese Model

We've heard a lot of stories from executives, administrators, and auditors alike on how they tried implementing a least privileged model without a PIM solution. Some folks used scripts to grant/remove administrator rights to the user; others used native settings such as Group Policy Files system and Registry ACL policies. We are not speaking badly of these admins and admittedly, have taken similar steps in the past; and in moderation, these do have a place.

The problem with utilizing this approach to completely address east privilege or least-privileged user accounts (LUA) is that you get into what we refer to as, "The Swiss Cheese Model." You inherently open up a number of security holes in your enterprise, not to mention risk breaking compatibility with applications, and create an incredible amount of work to maintain these policies and transfer this knowledge to other administrators. Following is an excerpt taken from a Microsoft Knowledge Base on this:

> "Extensive permission changes that are propagated throughout the registry and file system cannot be undone. New folders, such as user profile folders that were not present at the original installation of the operating system, may be affected. Therefore, if you remove a Group Policy setting that performs ACL changes, or you apply the system defaults; you cannot roll back the original ACLs.

Changes to the ACL in the %SystemDrive% folder may cause the following scenarios:

- The Recycle Bin no longer functions as designed, and files cannot be recovered.
- A reduction of security that lets a non-administrator view the contents of the administrator's Recycle Bin.
- The failure of user profiles to function as expected.
- A reduction of security that provides interactive users with read access to some or to all user profiles on the system.
- Performance problems when many ACL edits are loaded into a Group Policy object that includes long logon times or repeated restarts of the target system.
- Performance problems, including system slowdowns, every 16 hours or so as Group Policy settings are reapplied.
- Application compatibility problems or application crashes."

Establishing a least privilege environment or implementing a PIM solution is one of the only ways to solve this. Doing that correctly requires Secure Sam, Least Privilege Lucy, and Compliance Carl to come together.

Security Is a Team Sport and Least Privilege Is the Team Motto

In organizations that aren't sophisticated with measuring the value of risk, getting budget for security can be a tough gig. SC Magazine has an entire blog dedicated to an active running list of publicly known breaches, yet no matter how many examples you show, sometimes the logic that it will never be you is just a wishful-thinking phenomenon that can't be beat.

This is especially problematic when we talk about the risks of an accident, which requires systematic oversight to avoid. It would be so much cheaper and easier to just not make mistakes, right? So just don't screw up!

That must have been what the National Guard was thinking when they released the names, Social Security numbers, pay, and more for the 155th Brigade Combat Team by accident. The data was accidentally posted to an unsecure SharePoint site.

Details of the breach are still unknown, but the National Guard believes it was done inadvertently when uploading files to a new computer system. Let's make the leap and say that it had to be someone with administrative privileges who uploaded the database somewhere it shouldn't have been uploaded.

Who else would have access to 3,000 personal records and be moving that data around to support a new system?

Chances are it was a specific IT administrator that made the mistake, but the company did the right thing in not revealing who that person was. Hopefully, they took responsibility for systematic shortcomings that would allow the mistake of a single individual to cause so much harm.

It's a far cry from the case of the University of North Carolina, who attempted to fire their staff member who was responsible for a server that got breached by hackers. The organization decided this single individual was responsible for the utter and complete lack of security on the server.

Security is a team sport, but unlike soccer, you can't let the opposing team score a single goal. That means you can't let a player that trips lose the game for you.

Weighing In

All too often, the focus of attention can fall to what is going wrong, who was responsible, and what it cost, when information technology security is being discussed. By recognizing the Sams, Lucys, and Carls in your organization, and taking steps to support their activities, you will be investing in a secure and compliant future. This can also greatly limit your "misuse of privilege" liabilities.

We have analyzed numerous examples of these key insider hero personas along with supporting case studies and industry press. The primary lesson learned is understanding the need for separating rank from privilege and the value of implementing IT authorizations accordingly. There are several lessons we can take away from these experiences, but let's hear from our insider heroes:

Secure Sam:

Being the gateway for all users' administrator rights is a heavy responsibility, but one that is necessary in every organization. While not everyone needs the keys to the kingdom, everyone seems to think they do. Approving these privileges to those users who legitimately require them for their job functions is such a crucial step to the security of any organization, and not succumbing to political reasoning is equally important. The bottom line is this: understand the threats and protect all perimeters from threats. It can be so easy to focus on the outsider threat and ignore the very real reality that insider security is just as important. It's even easier to remain blissfully ignorant to attacks around us. It takes constant vigilance to protect precious company assets from both attackers outside the company walls as well as those that exist within the perimeters. It's vital to have the right individual in the role of CSO—one who has a big picture of his role, is willing to remain educated on new technologies, and has integrity with regard to his job and the quality of work he performs. Finding the right Security Sam for each individual enterprise is such a critical decision.

Least Privilege Lucy:

Managing the spectrum of privileges in an equally diverse set of platforms requires the juxtaposition of flexibility and rigidness. Whether it's Windows desktops, physical servers, virtual servers, databases, or cloud-based applications, users need a set of privileges that are specific to their individual jobs. While managing these user rights, you must also take certain things into account. The cost, for example, of IT personnel and the savings that can occur when privileges are appropriately delegated. Also, adapting rights and monitoring privileges for different network situations. Managing enterprise security is not a one-size-fits-all kind of thing, and a thorough analysis of required privileges is a vital exercise in ensuring said security. If users don't need to install software as part of their job function, then they don't need the administrative privileges that allow them to do that. Having the focus to create policies, then manage and monitor those policies, is critical to ensure against the over- and under-privileged user. It's also critical to understand human shortcomings in this process. It's absolutely not possible to manually program and upgrade this level of change while still meeting corporate governance and regulatory mandates. Knowing the proper tools and techniques plays a huge roll in this endeavor. Administration becomes an artifact of good decisions, good tools, and IT education. A lot of the time, this administration also happens in real-time.

Compliance Carl:

Being an auditor in today's ever-changing world of government compliance mandates is a role that is clearly outlined, especially when talking about user privileges. The way I see it, audits are simple: a company is compliant when its users have access to only those IT resources they are required to have access to. This access is based solely on job descriptions and necessity, and is outlined by industry-specific regulations. When analyzing a company for compliance, my assessment is predicated on what the entitlement reports show and whether the enterprise delegates privileges according to the mandates by which they're governed. Often, the difficulties arising from these mandates change and morph over time as the industry and associated regulations also change. Compliance, therefore, is a process and not just an event a corporation prepares for once. This applies to me in my role, as well, as an on-going education of regulations allows my point of view to remain refreshed and relevant. Continual training also allows for more thorough understanding of information technology best practices, as well as providing enough information for thorough audits to be performed. Knowledge is what keeps auditors objective, and it ensures audits rely on data, which is ultimately what keeps enterprises safe from both inside and outside attacks.

Supplementing Group Policy on Windows Desktops

"Another area of concern is that a user with local administrative privileges can install any application they wish on their desktop. This includes hack tools, virus-ridden applications, vulnerable applications, and non-licensed applications."

—Derek Melber, MSCE MVP and Author

In spite of an increasingly mobile workforce working flexible hours, the image of a "desktop" sitting on a Formica, faux cedar wood bureau, or workstation in a cubicle persists. But as we know full well, a desktop is not a machine required to be in a fixed location anymore. With technology what it is, that term is synonymous for a person (wherever they may be) that has access and is using Microsoft Windows.

Indeed, people are known to behave differently inside and outside of the office, where the cultures are different. Lines between professional and home life become blurred. People take the suit off at home and log in in their shorts, but that doesn't mean they should take their corporate hat off, as well. But what is the answer? Eliminating administrator rights without allowing for the elevation of certain job-necessary privileges is not the answer. Locking down a system is like asking everyone to raise his or her hand to go to the bathroom—it shows the downside of mistrusting human nature.

Trust is not a value that can be applied in a fixed dose; it has to be measured to meet the needs of the individual's role. Trust is a medicine that has to be applied carefully in prescribed doses based on role, policy, and circumstance. Just as you shouldn't gulp down an entire prescription when leaving the pharmacy assuming it will cure the problem in one go, you also can't just apply blanket privileges to users throughout your organization and expect that to solve your potential insider breach problem.

If you've read the marketing propaganda delivered by most operating system vendors, you have seen that they would like you to believe that their latest version will solve every problem known to exist just short of world hunger and world peace. It therefore behooves you to be aware of many glaring gaps that Windows exposes in privileged identity management (PIM).

Six Things You Should Know Before Migrating to MS Windows 7

Microsoft has done a great deal of exceptional work in improving Windows 7 over its predecessor, Windows Vista. Despite this improvement, glaring gaps in PIM still abound, requiring the security-conscious enterprise to consider Independent Software Vendors (ISVs) to eliminate desktop admin rights. The six things you should know before migrating to Windows 7 include:

1. *User Access Control (UAC) Security Vulnerability:* This exists when a user is logged in as *protected administrator*, in which case the default is to not notify users when changes are made to Windows settings, allowing users to "silently" elevate certain actions potentially leading to the introduction of malware.

2. *Registry and File System Virtualization Vulnerability:* Applications can write data into a virtual store, whereby other applications that need to use that data will no longer be able to access it.

3. *Application Compatibility Toolkit (ACT) Limitations:* ACT can tell you what applications require admin rights, but can do nothing to elevate rights for use of the applications.

4. *Virtualization (Med-V & App-V) Vulnerability:* Removing admin rights to a user on a PC but allowing them to open a window with admin rights to run a specific application for compatibility purposes will result in opening a security hole on that PC.

5. *AppLocker Limitations:* Requires the administrator to explicitly list every "legal" application, thus controlling what applications a user can use, but still requires admin rights at the user level if that application so requires.

6. *RunAs Administrator Vulnerability:* Only forces a UAC prompt when an application runs but doesn't elevate the rights for the user.

Things You Should Know About MS UAC

Microsoft (UAC) has been touted as the next great thing in desktop security, but does it really satisfy all you need in order to ensure security, compliance, and productivity? The things you should know about UAC include:

- For standard users, UAC is simply a RunAs operation. When prompted with UAC, a standard user is asked for credentials for an administrator account. When these credentials are entered, the application will run under that account and will no longer be able to access remote resources or save data to the correct profile.
- Microsoft does not offer logging or reporting for UAC. Auditing the use of UAC to discover what a user is doing with elevated privileges is a critical part of protecting the computer from unauthorized malware and malicious use.
- UAC has a security vulnerability in Windows 7 for users who log in as protected administrators. This vulnerability can only be mitigated if the user changes the UAC setting to its most secure level, which is the level used in Windows Vista. Alternatively, the vulnerability can be eliminated by removing administrator rights from the user.
- UAC dialogs cannot be supplemented with corporate legal text or customized warnings.

UAC has undergone a makeover from its debut in Windows Vista. Microsoft has reduced the number of prompts that UAC presents when a user is logged in to Windows. Microsoft implemented UAC to help prevent unauthorized changes to the operating system. UAC is designed to prompt a user when a task is performed in Windows that requires administrative privileges. For users who are logged in as a *protected administrator*, the prompt simply asks for consent.

If the protected administrator selects, yes, then the operation is allowed to continue with elevated privileges. The reason the user is called a "protected administrator is because he is actually operating with two tokens—one is a *standard user* token, the other is an *administrator* token. All tasks that the user performs are done as a standard user, until the user answers yes to a UAC dialog; once this happens, the user switches to an administrator token, and the task is elevated to administrator status.

Microsoft and security experts all agree that users should avoid operating as an administrator, with a full administrator token all the time, because it leaves the operating system extremely vulnerable to various security problems, including malware and malicious use.

With UAC, the user is notified whenever they elevate themselves to administrator for specific tasks to warn them of the potential for harm. The problem with this approach in corporate environments is that this strategy leaves the security decision up to the end user, which as we have said before, cannot be expected to be a saint or to be competent all of the time. Therefore, it is best to avoid configuring users as protected administrators, and make sure they are configured as standard users. Standard users have a different experience with UAC—instead of a simple prompt for consent, they are asked for a password for an administrative user.

If the standard user has the password for an administrator account, the process or application would run successfully. However, it would be running under a different account, without the security context of the actual end user. Essentially, this is an enhanced RunAs operation. Further, it only works if the user has an administrator password, or if someone else enters the administrator password for the user (*over-the-shoulder* credentials). Giving users administrator passwords will just lead to abuse, and over-the-shoulder credentials will only increase the load on the help desk.

Since the introduction of Windows Vista, organizations have been asking Microsoft to provide a way to manage a list of applications that would automatically elevate themselves and bypass the UAC prompts. Here is Microsoft's response to this request. According to Mark Russinovich, Technical Fellow at Microsoft; Inside Windows 7 User Account Control on technet.microsoft.com: "End users have been asking for Windows to provide a way to add arbitrary applications to the auto-elevate list since the Windows Vista beta... Windows 7, just like Windows Vista, doesn't provide such a capability."

Things You Should Know About MS AppLocker

AppLocker is a new and exciting technology in Windows 7 that can drastically improve desktop security in some organizations. AppLocker allows administrators to create a whitelist of all approved applications that are allowed to run on a computer; any other applications or executables would not be allowed to run. On the surface, this appears to be the security silver bullet; however, there are some things to be aware of when looking to AppLocker to help improve your security.

For example, if any of the applications that are on the AppLocker whitelist require administrator privileges, the user will need to be configured as a local administrator or they will, at the very least, still need an administrator password to answer UAC prompts. AppLocker cannot automatically elevate applications that are on the whitelist. If the user is configured as a local administrator, or has a local administrator password, it is easy to circumvent the controls that AppLocker provides.

The easiest way to circumvent the controls is by booting in Safe Mode and disabling the AppID Service. Because the user is an administrator, he would have full control to do this. Thus, removing administrator privileges from the user is critical in preventing the malicious user from circumventing these controls. If the user is not an administrator, AppLocker becomes much more effective, but organizations still need to find a way to deal with the applications that are on the whitelist that require administrator privileges.

There is also the question of the management of the whitelist. In smaller organizations that have relatively static environments, the combination of AppLocker and eliminating administrative rights is viable. Unfortunately, the whitelist scales with the size of the organization. As the company gets bigger, the whitelist gets bigger, and can become completely unmanageable very quickly. In larger organizations, it becomes nearly impossible to quickly react to users who need new applications placed on the whitelist.

When organizations choose to forgo the implementation of AppLocker for whitelisting, removing administrator privileges becomes even more important. Most applications require administrator privileges to install, and if organizations wish to prevent unknown applications from entering the environment, removing administrator privileges can add significant value.

Microsoft AppLocker has also been touted as the next best thing in desktop security (in addition to UAC), but does it really satisfy all you need in order to ensure security, compliance, and productivity? The things you should know about AppLocker include:

- AppLocker cannot elevate privileges for processes. It is designed to block or allow the execution of explicitly listed applications only.
- AppLocker does not allow organizations to remove administrator privileges. If you have applications that require administrator privileges, and those applications are on the AppLocker whitelist, the users will need to be configured as administrators.
- In order to make AppLocker secure, you must also remove admin rights from end users. If users are administrators, they can easily circumvent AppLocker policies and even disable the AppLocker service.
- AppLocker does not prevent users from accessing protected areas of the file system. If a user is an administrator and AppLocker is delivering a whitelist to the machine, the user can still modify critical areas of the file system.
- Managing an AppLocker whitelist can be difficult and cumbersome. This may not be suitable for large organizations with thousands of *line-of-business* applications.

Top Ten Reasons to Implement Least Privilege on Windows Desktops

Taking a more tongue-in-cheek approach to highlighting the types of privilege misuse that occurs daily inside most organizations, we thought that a top-ten list approach might appeal to you as well. How many of these have you seen throughout your organization?

#10—Sally in Sales will stop calling the help desk (at $30/call) every time she needs to change the system clock because she traveled to a different time zone and has standard user privileges.

#9—Andy the Auditor can get a full report of who has what entitlements instantly to satisfy compliance successfully, instead of taking weeks of manual effort.

#8—Ted in Tech Support won't have to drop everything to add a print driver to someone's PC if corporate policy actually permits them to do it themselves.

#7—Sid in Development won't be able to download potentially hazardous software onto his PC that in turn could infect the entire corporate network.

#6—Fiona the Secretary won't damage her PC configuration while trying to upgrade an application by accidentally "fat fingering" the wrong IP address.

#5—Bob, the VP of Marketing, won't crater the nightly backups by loading 120GB of music from his iTunes onto his corporate laptop.

#4—Alice in Human Resources will no longer be able to copy and sell private personnel data to supplement her income without the auditors being aware of her activities.

#3—Fred in IT won't be able to install a Trojan on the mission-critical server, bringing it down for four hours and costing the company over $1M in lost transactions, because he was passed over for a big promotion.

#2—Jack in Operations will no longer be permitted to download Active-X controls from online gaming web sites and spend hours of company time knocking over liquor stores in Grand Theft Auto.

#1—Charles Xavier III, the CEO, won't have the ability to screw up his laptop configuration accidently, indirectly, or even intentionally without a full event log being generated for audit, remediation, or recovery.

The "Do-Nothing" Approach

Daren Mar-Elia, Microsoft Group Policy MVP and founder of gpoguy.com and sdmsoftware.com, talks about organizations that try to get away without doing anything and hoping the problem never manifests. "I call this the bury-your-head-in-the-sand strategy. This is clearly one way to address a problem—by not addressing it. I still see a surprisingly large number of IT shops that take it for granted that their users run as administrators on their desktops. If they haven't yet had problems with malware or users wiping out their own systems, they will. Some shops will try to justify it by saying, 'well we have a lot of developers and they need to be administrators'."

Developers are indeed a challenge, but we would also argue they are a big risk group because they tend to download anything and everything from the Internet. Suffice it to say that we do not believe the Do-Nothing approach is sustainable in the long run. If Windows 7 and UAC aren't forcing you to address this problem head-on, then sooner or later you will need to confront it. If you need business justification to go to management to make the case for this, try some of these:

- Better security on your desktops and within your organization. If your company is even mildly regulated by a government organization, I can't imagine how you can get away with this for long. It's a PR nightmare waiting to happen!
- Lower Total Cost of Ownership (TCO) around managing your desktops as a result of less user futzing.
- More reliable end-user experience since installing untested, non-standard software and making user-driven tweaks can seriously impact desktop reliability.

Impact on the Help Desk

What's interesting here is that without exception, IT admins and help desk personnel, in organizations of all sizes, say they spend more than 1/4 of their time fixing problems caused by over-privileged users. In fact, in our conversations with organizations throughout the world, the average amount of time spent fixing these problems was 29% of all activities they are required to do. That means almost a third of their time is spent fixing problems, whether they be accidental errors (the so-called fat-fingered key stroke) or unintended errors, whereby simple actions such as downloading apps from the internet leaves the desktop susceptible to malware that can assume the user's administrator rights and use them to access the whole network.

According the Gartner, Inc.'s report, *The Cost of Removing Administrative Rights for the Wrong Users* (T. Cosgrove/April 2011), the primary difference between the two management profiles, "moderately managed" and "locked and well-managed," is user rights. The moderately managed profile assumes administrative rights are granted, while the locked and well-managed profile has them removed. The cost difference between the two profiles is $653 annually. Interestingly, 90% of the cost savings associated with the locked-down user is realized by the user, not IT. The user will spend less time fixing his or her system and doing other administrative tasks, because the PC is better managed.

They'd much prefer to be doing other things. Indeed, an overwhelming 90% of all our respondents to a survey of over 200 IT admins said they'd much rather automate the process of elevating privileges, and use the money they would save on either training staff or upgrading software. In essence, the experience of IT administrators and help desk operatives are legion; they want to spend more time improving user experience, with better training and software, and less time fighting fires (see Figure 4-1).

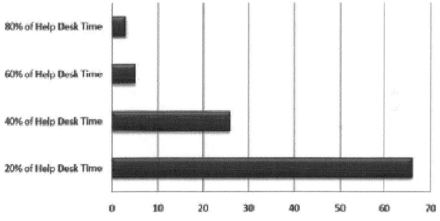

Figure 4-1. Most effective use of automated elevation of privileges

Fortunately, the fault is not the legacy applications. Businesses need not give up the applications they need to run business as usual. The fault is the lack of awareness of just how easy it is to automate the elevation of privilege user access at a granular level, based on the role definition of each employee. But let's not also forget that Windows itself can be a legacy app—as developers will have developed legacy apps based on older versions of Windows—at a time when knowledge of insider threat is great, and also the way MS vulnerabilities provide a back-door key to the network.

Microsoft Published Vulnerabilities

Microsoft and its partners regularly identify new security vulnerabilities in Microsoft software. In 2010, Microsoft published over 100 security bulletins documenting and providing patches for 256 vulnerabilities. In April 2011, BeyondTrust examined and analyzed all of the published Microsoft vulnerabilities in 2010 and all of the published Windows 7 vulnerabilities to date, allowing this report to accurately quantify the continued effectiveness of removing administrator rights at mitigating vulnerabilities in Microsoft software.

Key findings from this report show that removing administrator rights will better protect companies against the exploitation of:

- 75% of critical Windows 7 vulnerabilities reported by Microsoft to date
- 100% of Microsoft Office vulnerabilities reported in 2010
- 100% of Internet Explorer and IE 8 vulnerabilities reported in 2010
- 64% of all Microsoft vulnerabilities reported in 2010

Microsoft is to be lauded for releasing patches to known vulnerabilities each month. Vulnerabilities, however, take time to identify. Patches can take even longer to apply. During this down period, threats can damage a corporate network and gain access to sensitive information. A PIM solution that eliminates administrator rights from desktop users will substantially reduce the severity and/or prevent the exploitation of undiscovered or unpatched vulnerabilities. Enterprises should ensure that while administrative rights are removed to protect desktops from these vulnerabilities, users can also continue to operate effectively and with access to required applications.

The Wild West

Whenever we hear the phrase "Wild West," the first words that come to mind are old, insecure, and vulnerable. Any old western featuring Clint Eastwood or John Wayne depicts all of these descriptions.

And coincidentally, "Wild West" provides the perfect analogy for the way an enterprise's remaining legacy infrastructure interfaces with a Windows desktop environment. Though often overlooked, every IT administrator must face the challenge of managing legacy applications that simply will not run unless individual desktops are configured for administrator access. This remains a challenge in an enterprise Windows desktop environment, whether a company has 100 or 10,000 seats.

As we have detailed elsewhere, currently there are two options available to administrators:

- Option 1: Adopt best practice of removing administrative rights. Result: Overwhelms help desk with support calls and hampers productivity.

- Option 2: Grant users administrative privileges. Result: Can provide access points for malware, hackers, insider threats, and the less reported though still equally damaging fat-fingered unintentional error.

However, what has not been clear until now is that IT administrators and help desk operatives who choose Option 2 for the sake of productivity, and thus leave their desktop environment unnecessarily exposed, are not being cavalier or necessarily neglectful. The fact is they are left with no other choice because without their legacy applications running efficiently, productivity would come to a halt.

Survey Results Validate Problem

The conclusions of our recent survey of 185 IT administrators and help desk operatives who are collectively responsible for over 250,000 individual Windows desktops in Europe, the Middle East, Africa, and North America, which BeyondTrust published in May 2011 in a report titled *Legacy Applications and Least Privilege Access Management*, validate this problem. The results were revealing:

- Looking closer at the data, we found that in larger organizations with more than 2,500 active desktops, it was in-house custom applications (51% of respondents) and a range of 'other legacy apps' (40%) that force IT admins to elevate privileges to administrator or super user status.
- However, in organizations with fewer than 2,500 active desktops, it was the popular payroll software suite, Intuit QuickBooks (33% of respondents), and again 'other legacy apps' (50%), which most often forced IT administrators to elevate network access privileges to the more risky administrator or super user status.
- Survey respondents were invited to name which legacy app they were nominating when selecting Other, resulting in over 50 different apps nominated, with a number of respondents citing "too many to mention."
- This offers a revealing insight into the state of desktops today; namely, they are littered with applications, each requiring different configuration settings for different users, making effective access management practically impossible.

What we can conclude from this is that while the legacy apps may be different, the experience of all IT administrators and help desk operatives is uniform. Legacy applications make their lives difficult and consume a dispropor-tionate amount of their time, regardless of the size of the organization.

This points to the ubiquity of Windows and its inherent problems in elevat-ing privileged access based on company policy rather than the requirements of individual applications.

Perhaps the most revealing insight from our survey was that while we knew such legacy apps as Sage and QuickBooks caused problems for IT admins with over-privileged users, we hadn't anticipated just how many others there were. The types of legacy applications survey respondents identified ranged from the understandable to the completely absurd (company doesn't need it to run its business, and would violate compliance requirements if found with it.) and revealed over 50 different applications

Notable examples include:

- Old mainframe applications
- Software used for running an office (printer drivers) or the desktop itself (defragmenter)
- Third-party point-of-sale software provided to retailers
- Adobe and Flash software
- Technical applications, often used only by a handful of employees in oil, automotive, and chemical organizations, that still require the en-tire desktop to be set to administrator or super user status
- Applications downloaded by individual employees from the Web to help them do their job better, such as financial trading software, for example
- Applications downloaded and installed by employees for their own entertainment, such as iPhone applications, and in one instance, a Golf Course Game Application

Indeed, this paints a revealing picture of enterprise desktop environments today: they are littered with applications, each of which requires different configuration settings for different users, and makes effective access man-agement practically impossible.

Not surprisingly, many respondents said they had too many legacy applica-tions to mention. Indeed, is it any wonder that today's IT admins consider desktops the "Wild West," not just because of the overwhelm of managing access to multiple applications, but also because they never know what they're going to encounter on a user's workstation. One desktop manager reported: "We have limited control on what the end user can install and change on a desktop, and in many cases we have limited awareness of changes being made. In most cases, it's too late if a user installs malware and adware, leaving our desktop resources left fire-fighting problems."

Legacy applications architected before the concept of fine-graned privilege access can't be blamed in a wholesale manner for this problem though. Organizations need these applications to run business as usual, so implementing a least privilege solution is the best way to stem the requirement to completely rearchitect these applications.

Least Privilege, Architecturally Speaking

We've talked about least privilege throughout this book, but why should a desktop user care? Ultimately, a user needs admin rights on the desktop to:

- Run system tasks
- Install software (even active X controls from the Web)
- Run existing applications built to require admin privileges

An effective least privilege solution implemented for desktops will transparently plug into Active Directory and Group Policy in order to manage the elevation of privileges based on role and policy. This is what is called *least privilege* because you get the minimum amount of privilege in order to do a specific task only when it is needed. If the user has no privilege, then every attempt to do these tasks will be met with a UAC prompt asking for more privilege; if the user already has admin rights, then they are at risk for intentional, accidental, or indirect damage to their data (see Figure 4-2).

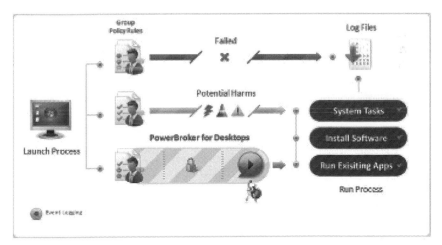

Figure 4-2. Architecture of least privilege.

Putting Least Privilege into Practice

Sometimes the best way to understand a conept as complex as least privilege for desktops is to examine a couple of real-word examples. Let's take a look at what one healthacare company and one university did to eliminate desktop admin rights and implement a least privilege solution.

Desktop Least Privilege in Production

Quintiles Transnational is a company that helps improve healthcare worldwide by providing a broad range of professional services, information, and partnering solutions to the pharmaceutical, biotechnology, and healthcare industries. Headquartered near Research Triangle Park, North Carolina, and with offices in more than 40 countries, Quintiles is a leading global pharmaceutical services organization and a member of the Fortune 1000.

As far as their IT environment goes, Quintiles Transnational manages over 13,000 end-user computers. The company wanted to remove the local administrative privileges from all their end-user accounts and run a least privilege user environment. The goal was to prevent employees from performing installations on their own, as well as running whatever software and applications they wanted. Unfortunately, Quintiles had a difficult time identifying a workaround that would allow applications requiring administrator privileges to run without the significant workload of writing custom install scripts or frequently visiting individual desktops to install software.

With Windows Active Directory installed and 13,000 computers running Windows XP, their least privilege solution was the perfect fit for the issues facing Quintiles. Security, compliance, and productivity were at the forefront of the company's needs, and this solution would enable them to create the least privilege environment they required while increasing end-user productivity. Quintiles continues to use it to elevate the permission level for the users who need to run authorized third-party applications, in addition to homegrown software, that require higher privileges than those to which the user is normally entitled.

Unpredictable Environments

Ian Short, Applications Infrastructure Manager for the University of Winchester, is part of the IT management team responsible for the operation of the IT environment across the university campus. The university predominantly runs a Microsoft site. All of the backend servers run Windows Server

2003 and 2008 within an Active Directory domain. Ian's department also supports over 1,500 Windows desktops on campus (all running Windows XP) that include over 7,000 user accounts. Many of these desktops include laptops used by remote employees in various locations. In addition, Ian and his team are responsible for 120+ applications, with a number of extra locally installed applications.

The challenge of managing user privileges in an environment full of students is complicated enough, but the dilemma only increases when you account for required applications. The team universally understood that they needed to eliminate administrator rights in order to decrease malware attacks and increase security. However, they also knew they couldn't lock down the entire network because of the 120+ applications they manage. "It became clear that in our environment something needed to be done," said Ian. "We were noticing a worrying growth in security risks and so managing user access became a priority."

With a least privilege solution, the University of Winchester has completely removed administrator rights among their users, while simultaneously providing adequate rights to perform the tasks that students and staff need. Some of the key uses include elevating privileges for 8 multimedia packages in their multimedia center, 24 applications on their desktops, and around half a dozen Windows functions, significantly decreasing the amount of time Ian and his team spend on support issues, which has significantly reduced cost as well.

Weighing In

Personal computers have proliferated beyond just the desktop, and with that has come an incredible management challenge. We've seen how too much privilege can potentially cause intentional accidental and/or indirect harm to the local data and possibly surrounding network. We've also discussed how too little privilege can cause sever help desk costs and declines in personal productivity. A least privilege solution is the only way to map personal privileges delegated by policy for compliance and governance satisfaction. But let's see what our insider heroes have to say

Secure Sam:

Least privilege, as we've talked about in this book before, is a simple and innately fundamental concept. It transcends every platform, making IT infrastructures secure in servers, databases, and desktops alike. In Windows desktops, least privilege makes particular sense as so many things can go wrong when users run with administrator rights. Too many times, however, least privilege is thought to be too complicated, and it gets ignored, brushed aside, or justified away. The reality of the situation is that this concept of allowing users to only access the IT resources that they absolutely need is worth whatever complications may arise. Especially on Windows desktops. Microsoft is constantly on the hunt for vulnerabilities to patch in their software, but the fact that there were over 250 in 2010 makes any additional security measures worth it in my eyes. When you take into account that removing administrator rights (or in other words, taking users to a least privilege model) mitigates the majority of Microsoft exploitations, the question shifts from "do I have to? It's so complicated!" to "how long does it take to get least privilege implemented." And rightly so—with 75% of critical Windows vulnerabilities and 100% of Microsoft Office vulnerabilities fixed by running users in standard user mode, IT decision makers are bypassing a significant amount of potentially devastating exploitations.

Least Privilege Lucy:

When weighing in on the principle of least privilege on Windows desktops, I can't help but focus on the impact such an effort has on the help desk. The help desk tends, in some cases, to be an expensive fix for problems that have no business existing at all. Users that have access to administrator privileges are scary because of all the ways those privileges can create gaping holes in an enterprises' security program. Whether it's if someone hijacks those credentials and steals information, or malware is unintentionally downloaded onto the desktop, or even if software was accidentally downloaded—these things all create messes that require the help desk to amend. It's an expensive way to handle the consequences of letting users run with whatever privileges are most convenient.

Compliance Carl:

The concept of trust with regard to an IT environment is kind of a strange thing. On the one hand, you can't base administrative rights on trust. On the other hand, you have to. While that may seem contradictory, the kind of trust I'm talking about is different in both cases. When someone is hired, an IT administrator can't just trust that he deserves a user account with admin privileges because HR performed a background check. Yes, he passed... but so what? The point is that trust as an emotion is useless in any IT environment. The kind of trust that does hold merit in your organization is a different kind of trust entirely… one that is founded in something bigger than emotion. The kind I was referring to in the second instance is the trust that comes carefully through policies, roles, and circumstances. It's the kind of trust that allows you to have administrator rights because you require them, not because I think you should have them. With the second kind of trust also must come follow-up. Monitoring privileges is a necessary part of trusting employees with them. Everyone must be accountable, and transparent insights into all activities while using those rights is a way for that trust to be further solidified. Roles must be continually evaluated, and adjustments must be made in order for least privilege to work on desktops.

Servers Are the Primary Target for Insiders and Hackers Alike

"As in previous years, nearly all data were breached from servers... This continues to be a defining characteristic between data-at-risk incidents and those involving actual compromise."

—Verizon RISK Team with US Secret Service,
2010 Data Breach Investigation Report

There is a significant distinction between the data on desktops described in the last chapter and the data on the server. To use another metaphor: if misusing desktop privilege can get you into the bank, then misusing server privilege is the equivalent of carte-blanche access to the bank vault. Indeed, in a secure and compliant server environment, end users are not entitled to the root password or even superuser status because organizations can no longer tolerate the security risks posed by intentional, accidental, or indirect misuse of privileges. However, organizations need to provide the admins of the plethora of heterogeneous servers across the enterprise with necessary privileges within specified guidelines to do their job safely.

Without a viable least privilege solution, the most common responses to this problem include sharing the root password, manually managing policy creation and change across each individual account, or being forced to implement inefficient and insecure alternatives. A server-based least privilege solution allows system administrators the ability to delegate privileges and authorization without disclosing the root password on Unix, Linux, and Mac OS X platforms. Additionally, all privileged access is recorded for audits, including keystroke information.

Servers Store the Good Stuff

That's right. Most anything of tangible asset value is most likely stored on a server somewhere within the perimeter of the enterprise. In today's world, that could even mean on a cloud platform, but that still constitutes the "enterprise perimeter." You probably have separate servers for e-mail, transaction databases, your financial information, and possibly a contact management system—any one of which if compromised could cost your company significantly in tangible expense and lost productivity.

Server Breaches in the News

If you have 1 of 44,000 inactive Mozilla accounts, you may have received a belated Christmas present in December 2010, when the company sent out notifications of a potential leak of their account information. In this case, the company was able to reassure those users there was virtually no possibility of any harm to them.

However, what's interesting about the incident is that one can only presume it ties back to a very specific administrator who on a very specific day and time made a mistake and put the database on the wrong server. Something we see with surprising frequency.

Now put yourself in Mozilla's shoes. If this happened to you, would you know which IT staff was responsible? What would you tell the CEO? Would a witch hunt ensue and how would that impact the department?

The incident highlights once more that the IT staff can and do make terrible mistakes that can cost millions in breaches, notifications, and more. Because IT staff has such deep access to the IT systems themselves, a single logistical mistake can have deep security implications.

The incident highlights why organizations need processes and systems in place that account for the very real possibility of errors by IT staff. In other words, you need to monitor and record the actions of individual administrators and remove blanket root access.

This not only creates accountability for individual staff to not make a mistake in the first place, but avoids the witch hunt when it happens. Employees need to know that if they make mistakes, intentionally or accidentally, the company will know who it was. This, in and of itself, remains the cornerstone of deterring good people from doing bad things. If you know your actions are being recorded, you are more likely to only do what you have been asked to do.

Black Market for Server Data

The economy of cyber crime is all too real—and too enticing. No longer sequestered to dark alleys and seedy bars, data thieves have almost unlimited options to market their ill-gotten wares to potential buyers. What this means to employers and organizations: the temptation to access and "appropriate" sensitive data may be too great for some to resist.

So just how easy is it for cybercriminals to sell data? Shockingly easy.

Although the sale of stolen information often takes place completely underground in secret, closed to the public credit forums, people who want to join these groups can locate them quite easily. Once vetted by forum administrators to ensure they are not from law enforcement, they are invited into the network to market and distribute their wares. According to Sue Walsh at AllSpammedUp.com in July 2009: "The personal information of at least 4 million Britons and a whopping 40 million others, most of whom are Americans, is being bought and sold online. This includes usernames and passwords, credit card details, bank account numbers and more."

And individuals need not even proactively seek out to divest an employer of sensitive, valuable data. Today, recruiters actively target individuals with local or specific data types, going so far as to even create job postings with such criteria as "an established relationship with local banks" as a prerequisite for crime family consideration.

The ease with which individuals can locate black market buyers of data should scare every employer who provides mid- to low-level access to any type of sensitive information. Like some bizarro-world eBay, many of these markets actually have incentive packages. Competing prices, additional services, free trials, money-back guarantees, and terms and conditions are all offered. Prices for data are qualified like any other commodity: data is priced based on the domain, if the account belongs to a real person, and how popular it is. It can depend on the number of followers, how commercial the niche is, and if the data is real or bot-generated. Prices for online banking and payment systems dependent on account verification.

To make matters worse, the cyber-crime black market, which has traditionally centered on distributing bank and credit-card details stolen from users around the world, has diversified its business model since 2010, and now sells a much broader range of hacked confidential information, including bank credentials, logins, passwords, fake credit cards, and more.

So, while CSOs struggle to combat an ever-evolving crime organization that morphs and changes in a nanosecond, it may be the guy in the cube next to you seeking to supplement his bank account who could exact the most damage to your database.

The Architecture of Server Least Privilege

Implementing a least privilege environment across servers is a bit different than that of desktops. Not just because of the operating system requirements, but the very nature of server administration. Ultimately, an admin needs least privilege instead of full superuser rights on the server or they may:

- Share the root password to perform tasks
- Manually manage policies across disparate Linux systems (such as Red Hat and SuSE)
- Store logs insecurely
- Transmit data unencrypted

Least privilege on a server isn't dissimilar to implementing least privilege on a desktop (see Figure 5-1). The fundamentals of a policy engine, an authorization broker, and a log server still exist. The fundamental difference is that servers tend to be more command-line–driven for administration, while desktops tend to be GUI–driven. Command requests are therefore submitted in order for the least privilege engine to do its magic. It is also important to note that the propensity for error is greater with command-line interfaces than with GUIs due to the possibility of missing parameters or mis-typing specific command qualifiers. So, the need for policy oversight at a keystroke level also becomes a critical success factor when implementing least privilege in server environments. Here is a typical flow:

1. A user submits a request to run a command.

2. The Master Host validates it against security policy files to either approve or reject it.

3. An accepted request is executed on the Run Host as a privileged user.

4. All activity is logged and recorded by the Log Servers.

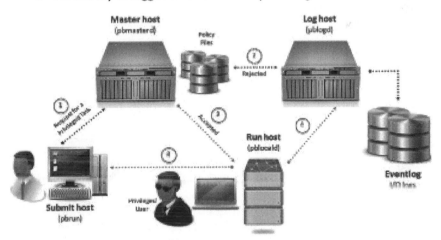

Figure 5-1. Architecture of least privilege

Of WikiLeaks and Servers

We're used to the media getting sidetracked by the content of data breach stories, rather than how they happened. Not surprisingly, then, the WikiLeaks story of early 2011 is no different. With thousands of sensitive diplomatic dispatches to wade through, reporters will likely have enough information to keep them busy for quite some time. Of course, there is a place for this analysis, and yet not for the first time, another opportunity has been lost to pinpoint the weakest link in better securing data.

Although it's likely the White House attempts to identify the weakest link, they also use smokescreens to divert attention from the content of the leaks to those responsible for handling classified information in a surprisingly effective manner.

> *"...create a 'security assessment team' to review the implementation of procedures to safeguard such information, a review to include making sure that no employee has access to information beyond what is necessary to do his or her job effectively."*

By pointing to the management of privileges as the cornerstone of best security practice, they recognize the delicate balance that must be struck between ensuring productivity on the one hand, and security on the other. Bottom line: by leveraging access based on job definition and the privileges that job requires, rather than seniority, organizations will ensure no employee has access to information "beyond what is necessary to do his or her job effectively." It's worth reiterating that CEOs don't need access to servers running the network, while the IT help desk doesn't need access to the CFO's domain.

However, what the White House doesn't say is just how rife access to information "beyond what is necessary to do his or her job effectively" (overprivilege access) is.

According to a multi-industry survey conducted by the Ponemon Institute in early 2011, 79% of government IT practitioners admitted to having too much access to information resources that aren't pertinent to their role in the organization.

The report's authors rightly say this may be because government organizations cannot keep pace with access change, which happens continuously, and indeed, 75% of those surveyed said that they could not respond quickly enough to such changes. 60% also do not immediately check user requests against security policies before access is approved and assigned.

This speaks of a world in which access, when it is controlled, is still elevated manually by request (or not) from individual users. This leaves network access open to abuse, either through error, or, as is the case with WikiLeaks, from employees set on making mischief.

Far better government organizations consider some kind of automated privilege access lifecycle management, which elevates access, based on the pre-prescribed role definition of each employee, and keeps a log to show who went where, when, and for how long.

This doesn't, by any stretch, prevent data breaches from happening. If someone has privilege access, they can still steal or leak sensitive data. As suggested at the beginning of the chapter, what good least privilege solutions can do, however, is provide a strong deterrent, because good least privilege solution means access is not just leveraged on a "needs must" basis, it is logged too.

In organizations where everyone has full administrator access to the network, determining who might have leaked data would be like looking for a needle in a haystack. For organizations running good least privilege systems, it's possible to narrow down the possibilities of who had access to what and when to fewer individuals. With that in mind, employees might think again before blowing the whistle. This is especially true for server-based least privilege solutions where keystroke logging will record everything done at a granular level, whereas desktop least privilege usually just tracks at an event level.

WikiLeaks and WikiWar

How much press will we have to endure on the significant problems created by WikiLeaks and the public lynching of those who perpetrate these leaks before we realize that if you give someone an inch (excessive admin rights), they will take a mile (misuse that privilege)?

To use a metaphor: if I sneeze, will you give me a tissue and send me on my way? Will you give me cold medicine? How about allergy medicine? Without knowing the cause, the "disease," then reacting to the sneeze, "the symptom," will ultimately result in a response that may be overkill or underkill.

Some journalists do get it. Mike Martin at TechNewsWorld published an insightful story titled *WikiLeaks Wrangling May Be Escalating Into Cyberwar*. He rightly points out that "the WikiLeaks controversy could be devolving into a wiki-war."

So why is it that every journalist seems to be focused on the symptom (the leak), instead of the disease (the intentional misuse of privilege caused by excess admin rights)?

Implementing a privilege identity management (PIM) solution and eliminating admin rights from servers, desktops, network devices, virtual servers, and cloud environments is a strong move in the right direction to ensure that everyone in your organization only has access to what they should have based on corporate policy. This ensures governance and regulatory compliance and limits the potential for other leaks from your organization.

To exacerbate the situation, we've seen it described as everything from a WikiWar to Wiki Gaga, and yet most writers are still forgoing that if you give someone permission to do something, they will inevitably do it. In this case, we are once again referring to the IT privileges granted to individuals and associated technologies to monitor and control what these people are doing. Or the lack thereof.

By implementing a least privilege solution, you are taking the first step toward better IT management and a method of policing corporate governance. The root cause (excuse the pun) should ultimately be recognized as the misuse of privilege.

Implementing a PIM solution can allow you to:

1. Eliminate admin rights across servers, desktops, network devices, virtual, and cloud environments to prevent anyone from having omnipotent access to those resources.

2. Control levels of privilege for those resources to ensure the elimination of the misuse of privilege.

3. Log all events and administrator activities so that in the event of a breach or a misuse of privilege, you can remediate that breach.

4. As today's t-shirt points out, you can focus on the variables that positively affect your business growth instead of being at war with your user community or wind up in the press.

One solution that seems to be prevalent in some circles to use the open source solutions available to implement least privilege. This solution is called Sudo and was created by Bob Coggeshall and Cliff Spencer around 1980 at the Department of Computer Science at SUNY/Buffalo.

Why Do You Sudo the Way You Do?

Sudo has been one of the Unix/Linux administrator and self-designated geek's best friend for the last two decades, but it probably isn't right for your enterprise. For one thing, it's open source software, which means no one company can be held accountable for bug fixes, enhancements, or any liability resulting from flaws in design. Of course, being software guys, we naturally lean toward licensed code and cover the subject of licensed code versus freeware (see Figure 5-2) a little later in this chapter.

Indeed, many IT professionals believe that by implementing Sudo across their enterprise, they are now protected from the intentional, accidental, and indirect misuse of privilege. Unfortunately, that is not the case, as anyone with a browser and the keywords "Sudo breach," "Sudo tricks," or "Sudo hack: will learn. If you have three minutes to spare, there is even a YouTube video to show you how in step-by-step instructions for the Guy Hawkes Hack.

In the land of Unix and Linux systems administration, nothing seems to elicit such polar love and hate as does the use of Sudo for root rights elevation.

> *Pro Sudo:* The single biggest cry for support of Sudo tends to be "it's Free!" or "it came with my OS". Suffice it to say that Sudo has been in use since "around 1980", when it was developed by Bob Cogge-shall and Cliff Spencer and made available as open source software. Currently it is actively developed and maintained by Todd Miller and distributed under a BSD style license. The second biggest cry for support is "but it passed my last audit."

> *Con Sudo:* The amount of effort required to configure and maintain, especially since Sudo requires separate Sudoers files on each server instead of centralizing policy management and reporting. Nothing is truly free when it comes to freeware. Periodic review of Sudoer files alone can be so time consuming as to potentially miss an audit or inhibit other more pressing priorities. Yes, you can create a "Master Sudoers" file, but once it is copied to a server, it could be edited independently. It is also very difficult to map master entitle-ment reports to actual Sudo commands across the extended enter-prise, especially in a changing environment. And finally, as Google just discovered, whenever you have an open source solution, the possibility of malware injection escalates significantly.

Ultimately, you will need to decide whether or not good is good enough long-term and uncover what the true cost or "free" is to your organization. So, why do you Sudo the way you do?

One of the problems with Sudo is the ease with which it can be deployed haphazardly, without a lot of forethought, to address a particular day's privi-lege challenges. Mary needs to manage the office printers. John needs to re-set passwords for people in the business unit he supports. Janice needs to perform server maintenance. The admin that restricts access to the root password without a ready alternative will become popular indeed, and not in a good way.

Enter Sudo as that ready alternative. Privileges can be granted quickly, independently, with minimal effort. But before you know it, one privilege request processed on top of another leads to a hodgepodge of poorly maintained Sudoer files, all hosted on local servers with local log files and no audit trail to speak of. Better than the proliferation of the root password? Sure, but by how much? Figure 5-2 shows the primary differences between freeware and/or open source software versus products licensed and supported by commercial vendors.

Freeware	Licensed Software
Statically defined permissions	Rich policy language for complex procedural logic
No true "shell" functionality	Integrated "shell" variants of Korn and Bourne shells
Event logging of input only	Full keystroke logging of input and resulting output
Log files in clear text with identity information exposed	Encrypted audit trail prevents alteration and erasure
Config files must be manually copied to each local machine for any change	Scalable, maintainable and fault-tolerant in large heterogeneous environments
Default run user if "root"	No access unless explicitly granted
Open source software not maintained by any single entity	Full support 24/7 and maintenance upgrades

Figure 5-2. Differences between licensed software and freeware.

Now consider the compliance implications. Many companies have standard compliance policies for Sudo, most of which require routine inspections of each Sudoer file to ensure that permissions granted to each user are appropriate. Not an easy task when the server count is in the hundreds or more. Many organizations find that a spot check of Sudoer files reveals permissions for users who have long since left the company—a guaranteed audit violation.

In reality, there is no substitute to carefully creating a privilege delegation strategy and designing a rollout plan that ensures security and compliance while minimizing the impact on users. While you can do this with Sudo just as you can with commercial tools, the fact is that commercial tools provide better guardrails around deployment and more sophisticated native features, such as encrypted logging and centralized policy stores, for enabling security protections and ease of maintenance. And the most robust ones provide an easy path to proving compliance, a challenge most administrators of Sudo deployments find all too formidable.

Sudo Vulnerabilities

From 2010 through Q1 2011, the Department of Homeland Security (DHS) released ten vulnerability alerts for Sudo with a medium or high severity rating. DHS' National Vulnerability Database (NVD) is the US government repository of standards-based vulnerability management data represented using the Security Content Automation Protocol (SCAP).

Figure 5-3 illustrates the types of vulnerabilities that have appeared since 2010 on DHS' NVD, and the number of times these vulnerabilities appeared among the ten Sudo alerts. It is important to note that multiple types of vulnerabilities have appeared in one alert (that is, Allows Disclosure of Data). This data was retrieved from http://web.nvd.nist.gov/view/vuln/search.

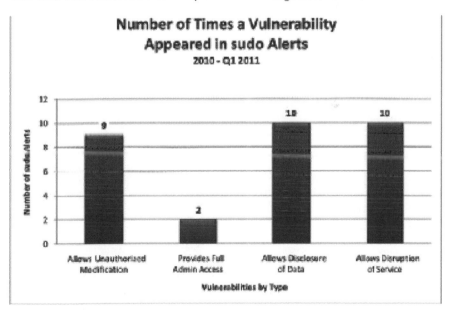

Figure 5-3. Sudo vulnerability alerts

What's really interesting about this chart is the subtext that implementing Sudo actually introduces some potential for security breach and insider threats than not implementing it at all. It also doesn't make it any less likely that good people will do bad things, as it simply exacerbates the complacent approach to PIM inherent in most organizations. It could even be construed as a "sloppy" approach to attempting least privilege given its open source nature.

Top Ten Reasons to Implement Least Privilege on UNIX and Linux Servers

Taking a more tongue-in-cheek approach to highlighting the types of privilege misuse that occurs daily on servers inside most organizations, we thought that a top-ten list approach might appeal to you as well. How many of these have you seen throughout your organization?

> *#10*—Sam, the CSO, can now sleep nights knowing that excess privileges will no longer be responsible for failing a SOX, HIPAA, PCI, DSS, GLBA, or FDCC and FISMA audit (even though he isn't required to even deal with the last two).

> *#9*—Andy the Auditor can get a full report of who has what entitlements instantly to satisfy compliance successfully, instead of taking weeks of manual effort.

> *#8*—Ted in Tech Support won't be able to reset file and directory permissions on any Linux server he has admin rights to so liberally that anyone with a login can access confidential data just because it makes his job easier.

> *#7*—Sid in Development won't be able to download Apache applications or any other unauthorized open source "tools" potentially injecting malware into the corporate network.

> *#6*—Fiona and Felix, our new server administrators, won't make one, or more, of the Ten Mistakes New Linux Administrators Make.

> *#5*—Vito, the ever-industrious programmer, will no longer be able to code suid root binaries into his programs, allowing programmatic access beyond what is allowed by corporate policy or regulatory requirements.

#4—Alice in IT will no longer be responsible for DNS misconfiguration errors, as her role won't facilitate this level of admin privilege.

#3—Fred in IT won't be able to install a Trojan on the mission-critical server, bringing it down for four hours and costing the company over $1M in lost transactions, because he was passed over for a big promotion.

#2—Sarah, the CIO. will no longer have to hide Unix and Linux root credentials in a sealed envelope in her office safe and deal with a manual check in/check out process.

#1—Tony, the Palo Alto Linux administrator. will no longer be able to wear that ratty old T-shirt with the slogan *"Bow before me, for I am root"* any longer.

More Server Breaches in the News

Health information exchanges (HIEs) is the latest buzz phrase to hit the compliance marketplace. In a recent post, blogger phiprivacy.net reported on the opinions of top IT experts about the top patient healthcare information trends for 2011.

Among a clear indication of increased breaches, imposition of fines and other regulatory action, and the implementation of new laws, the experts identified the launch of new HIEs as the main driver of change in enforcing increased security and privacy.

Although HIEs have a noble purpose In making it easier for healthcare professionals to access patient information electronically across multiple organizations within a region, community, or hospital system in order to provide more efficient and effective care, the risks of increased exposure to data breach remain high.

Not only do the experts point out that many HIEs will be launched by inexperienced and understaffed organizations, they will be launched in an industry (healthcare) that has consistently failed to keep pace with data security best practices and governance.

This is clearly a case of healthcare organizations putting the cart before the horse. In an ideal world, the horse is an efficient IT system, and the cart is the service that system is able to provide to the end user.

Trying to improve the cart without upgrading the horse from the old nag it currently represents is likely to leave healthcare organizations even deeper in the mire. Best practice for healthcare data security is no different from any other industry.

Indeed, sensitive user access control, based on least privilege role definition, remains the cornerstone of HIPAA compliance and will require the elimination of admin rights to prevent the misuse of privilege.

Case Study: Replacing Sudo in a Production Environment

CETREL S.A. (www.cetrel.lu), a leader in advanced electronic payment technology, expert in electronic transfers, and a trusted partner for electronic payment offers, experienced significant compliance and auditing challenges using Sudo to manage their IT environment.

Nicolas Debeffe, head of operational security at CETREL, is responsible for overseeing CETREL's security operations, which includes their complex IT environment. For the last several years, Mr. Debeffe's security team had been using Sudo to manage their critical Unix/Linux assets and trace any access from CETREL's support teams to applicative or generic users.

While Sudo initially seemed to manage CETREL's IT environment, they soon discovered that there was an imminent need to find a simpler and more secure method to manage access and accountability to generic users.

"As we have been continually adding Unix and Linux servers to our environment, as required for our operations, it was clear Sudo raised significant red flags over the adequate security over our logs required by PCI DSS mandates," said Nicolas Debeffe.

"Productivity was being hindered, as reviewing Sudo logs required accessing every server individually. Furthermore, Sudo logs were alterable by the super user and the Sudo configuration time required by system engineers was simply unacceptable," added Debeffe.

This example is a very common and real challenge for security managers globally, and the faster organizations are cognizant of such red flags, the faster they can implement preventative measures from a strategic and compliant perspective.

Vulnerability Scanning Requires Least Privilege

Many companies still rely heavily on vulnerability scanning to ensure outsiders aren't getting in. Root-level access for authenticated scanning is an important part of vulnerability management scanning and required for policy compliance scanning. This creates another open doorway for the misuse of privilege in your organization. Yep, yet another account that has unlimited access to corporate resources under the guise of "being more compliant."

The good news is that some industry leaders in vulnerability management and policy compliance scanning recognize this and are doing something about it. Specifically, they have partnered with least privilege vendors to create a more secure scan.

Most vulnerability scanning vendors use a Software-as-a-Service (SaaS) model to automate the process of vulnerability management and policy compliance via remote authenticated scanning without the use of agents. Using a least privilege solution in combination with this enables system administrators to delegate privileges and authorization without disclosing root passwords, preventing misuse of privileges on desktops and servers in heterogeneous IT environments. This integration enables you to use least privilege root delegation functionality for authenticated vulnerability and compliance scans on Unix systems. This allows system administrators to better manage access while scanning their environments as they can delegate privileges and authorization and record all interactions, including keystroke information, for auditing purposes.

Patching Needs Least Privilege

A report came out in early 2011 highlighting vulnerabilities in NASA's IT that could have impaired critical space missions or leaked sensitive information.

Using the NASA CIO's own words, *The Network World* story by Tim Greene points the finger in the same mistaken direction most anyone would as a reflexive response: the lack of an ongoing program to identify and patch vulnerabilities. But the article itself also presents the very obstacle to that. NASA was/is patching software routinely, but there's just too much to patch, too many updates, too often that need to be implemented too quickly. Mistakes and overlooked vulnerabilities are bountiful. What about vulnerabilities that aren't discovered yet, were just discovered but not patched, or are known but overlooked. Is there no room for error?

The report states the agency has over 190 IT systems and projects that include assets that control the Hubble Space Telescope, the Space Shuttle, and the International Space Station among others and describes previous breaches where extremely sensitive information had been leaked by sophisticated attacks. In one case, malware was allowed to spread and make 3,000 unauthorized connections to IP addresses all over the globe. The report blames "inadequate security configurations."

This is another example of the indirect misuse of privilege discussed at length in Chapter 2. Anyone who still has admin privileges is susceptible to having those credentials hijacked and malware planted.

What the NASA story is missing in the mainstream media is that running around patching vulnerabilities everywhere they can be found is only half the solution. It's like a game of whack-a-mole—you're never done and you'll always be too late to at least one. Companies need to reduce their risk exposure even under the assumption that some vulnerabilities will be leveraged—and they will.

Privilege Identity Management System Logs Help Spot Other Security Weaknesses

Those detailed compliance logs you have been generating are a gold mine of information. Analyzing large amounts of data is a growing trend. From Google to Walmart, companies are building their strategies on complex models and algorithms.

You can use systems logs not just to look for patterns that indicate a security threat, but those same patterns can show where security and other procedures such as improper configurations of new systems are hurting productivity. Finding those patterns can help uncover opportunities to better train, simplify procedures, and uncover best practices that not everyone is following. And once those best practices are discovered, you can use controls to ensure that best practices are being followed.

Realizing that value requires a data analysis strategy and a strategy for how to engage the organization in using that analysis. Your data analysis strategy needs to consider the roles of monitoring, logging, and reporting, as well as when and how to combine data from different sources. Single silos of data are simpler to use, but correlating data across silos provides more powerful insights. Ultimately, you will need both, but your data analysis strategy needs to focus on providing insights your organization can act on. And that's where you need to consider how to engage your people in using the data.

Weighing In

Servers can be the holy grail of targets for insider villains, and as such need to be dealt with specifically and diligently. We've discussed how they are the primary attack point and for good reason: this is where the most valuable data is usually stored. We showed how some organizations attempt to implement least privilege using an open source solution that may open other vulnerabilities. What we think is most interesting is the magnitude of the impact caused by the lack of least privilege implemented In server environments and the hundred of millions of dollars and potential jail time that can be associated with insider breaches.

Let's hear from our Insider Heroes:

Secure Sam:

One of the responsibilities I have (and candidly, the one that stresses me out the most) is making sure people within my organization have the right amount of privileges. I've seen it all—between the classic accident-prone employees who are always downloading malware without knowing it to the ones who are a bit too cavalier with passwords—it seems like it's a battle I will always have to fight. The idea of least privilege is crucial in this battle, especially on our servers. The information stored on the servers of our company hold mission-critical data. It's not data I can afford to risk because of a mistake. My IT staff has such entrenched access to the IT system, one mistake can have catastrophic results. Because of this, access to company resources and assets are restricted to a need-to-know basis. All users have access to only the information they absolutely need to do their job productively. No one has root access—a mistake at the root level is simply not acceptable. We also have processes that monitor and log all activity in the event that something does happen. Especially with servers, these measures must be taken to ensure the highest level of security and compliance.

Least Privilege Lucy:

There are a lot of security things that can go wrong, especially in large enterprises. Particularly in server environments, it's paramount that data protection is taken seriously—in both word and in action. Everyone says they're concerned with security and that it's their top priority, but when I go to work and have to put out fire after fire, it becomes very obvious that what users say and what they do are on completely different planes. This is why least privilege is so important. And not just least privilege, but a solution that centrally delegates privileges so I don't have to hassle with Sudo or other open source command lines. Here's an example of how this is effective. Take my biggest pet peeve: a user with access to the root password sharing it with other users who are not cleared to have that information. Not only is this a huge breach of security, but it is also not compliant with federal regulations to which we are held. With a least privilege solution, no users have the root password; therefore, it remains safe from those who don't need it. Instead, those requiring root access for their job functions are automatically delegated that privilege by elevating the individual task. With so much on the line and with so many data breaches in the media, this is a safeguard that is necessary.

Compliance Carl:

Compliance on servers is crucial, as that is where the most critical of information is stored. There are regulation mandates in place to protect this data, and in most companies I visit, it seems like this concept isn't fully understood. Yes, IT administrators get that keeping servers secure is paramount to the company's IT health, but if they fully grasped the concept, I wouldn't see open source software ruling the policies and privileges of the company's secure information. Even if the files are regularly inspected (which is required by various regulations), there is too much left to human error for that to be a viably secure protocol. Several things make this a challenge, which was talked about before, but as they are real struggles in real IT environments, I thought it prudent to reiterate a couple of them here. First of all, with open source software like Sudo, each individual server has a unique file that must be analyzed and reviewed. This becomes an enormous task when there are a lot of servers in an enterprise. Secondly, because the command policies are so heavily code-based, it is time-consuming and expensive to manage privileges in this way. Sudo has its place, but it is definitely not in large companies. The best option is this: a privilege delegation strategy that centrally manages privileges, logs activity, and ensures security while saving time and productivity.

Protecting Virtual Environments from Hypervisor Sabotage

"Virtualization is not inherently insecure. However, most virtualized workloads are being deployed insecurely."

—Neil MacDonald, VP and Gartner Fellow, Gartner Inc.

Organizations moving their physical server infrastructure onto virtual platforms for cost savings are finding their virtual hosts and guests are now open to new security and non-compliance risks. Workloads shifted to virtualized platforms to realize operational cost efficiencies are done so at potentially high security costs if proper security policies and tools are not established prior to implementation. As if we didn't need to state the obvious, virtualization doesn't make it any less likely that good people will do bad things.

Administrative access to the server hypervisor/VMM layer and the administrative tools used to access these layers must be tightly controlled to maintain a strong security posture. When multiple resources with many different levels of privileged access are consolidated onto a single physical server without sufficient workflow protocol, separation of duties for network and security controls could be compromised and security policies circumvented.

A least privilege solution provides granular privilege identity management (PIM) across guest operating systems as well as hypervisor hosts through a single centralized management console. Privileged access security risks are mitigated, compliance requirements met, and organizations can adopt virtualization with confidence.

A least privilege solution also provides a cost-effective dedicated solution to centrally address risks from unmanaged administrative privileges in virtualized datacenter environments. In a secure and compliant environment, users privileged access to virtual resources are managed to give them access to only what they need to do their job.

Protecting virtual environments is a difficult and tedious task. On one hand, privileges in this setting must be granularly managed to ensure complete security. On the other hand, it takes less time and energy to allow users to operate with unmanaged privileges in virtualized datacenter environments. Fortunately, there is an answer to this double-edged question, and it allows for the risks in said environment to be mitigated.

Virtual Theft

A key factor to consider when approaching virtualization security is that the hypervisor is always going to be a high-value target due to its control over the entire virtual environment. The misuse of privilege at the hypervisor level can present the following risks:

A hypervisor breach would allow "authorized access" to all hosted/virtualized workloads. Essentially finding the "key to the hypervisor" gives you the "keys to the kingdom." While root password access in a server environment gives you the keys to the vault inside the bank, the hypervisor gives you access to multiple vaults inside the bank. Unmanaged administrative access to the hypervisor also facilitates two other potentially damaging problems:

- Incorrect or unauthorized configurations magnify risks
- "Virtual sprawl" due to lack of policy enforcement.

Hypervisors must be considered mission-critical and secured appropriately, just like operating systems, and require security because of the risks to the system and applications. Typically, users are simply given administrator rights to perform configuration or policy changes to the virtual environment.

Even if mounting disks is to be allowed, there are built-in workflows to capture policy requests and approvals for that command. Additionally, workflows can be set up to alert a manager if the mount command is used. Finally, a least privilege solution creates an indelible searchable keystroke trail, which would capture all activity that the administrator conducts during the mounting.

Committing virtual theft (Figure 6-1) isn't a difficult thing to accomplish without least privilege management of the hypervisor.

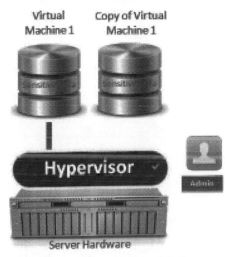

Figure 6-1. Committing virtual theft

Step 1) Administrator with root credentials on hypervisor has access to "Virtual Machine 1" with sensitive data.

Step 2) Administrator copies virtual machine1 to get an exact replica "copy of Virtual Machine 1," containing sensitive data.

Step 3) Administrator kills "Virtual Machine 1" copy, and mounts the disk image.

Step 4) Administrator is able to navigate to and gain full access to sensitive data on the mounted disk image, unnoticed, while "Virtual Machine 1" is still running fine.

A least privilege solution can prevent this scenario by disallowing the administrator to use the mount command, while allowing her to use other commands required to carry out her job effectively.

The federal government has even recently taken note of such threats, as shown in an October 2010 DarkReading article titled *Pentagon's Insider Threat Push Offers Lessons for Enterprises*. The research arm of the Pentagon, known as the Defense Advanced Research Projects Agency (DARPA), put out a call last week for better methods of detecting employees just before or after they go rogue and misuse their privileges. "Unfortunately, virtual insider threats have been largely identified due only to incompetence on the part of the perpetrator or by accident," says Peiter "Mudge" Zatko, the manager in charge of the program at DARPA.

If you search on "virtual guest vulnerability" in your favorite search engine and filter to video results only, you will find a step-by-step guide demonstrating how to do this as well as how to protect against this form of virtual information theft.

Desktop Virtualization

Virtualization has become a hot buzzword over the past several years, and for good reason. With the introduction of Virtual PC several years ago, and now with Windows XP Mode, Microsoft Enterprise Desktop Virtualization (Med- V) & Application Virtualization (App-V), Microsoft is no stranger to virtualization.

With all these technologies, it is easy to understand that there is significant confusion in the market about what virtualization means for privilege management, specifically the ability for virtualization to help with the removal of administrative rights from users. While virtualization can add enormous value in many areas, many organizations will rely on virtualization to help specifically with application compatibility problems.

For example, if an organization cannot get an application to run on Windows 7, even after trying to shim the application with the Application

Compatibility Toolkit, the ability to virtualize the application with one of the technologies listed earlier is available.

Unfortunately, virtualization does not help with the elimination of administrative privileges; it simply shifts the problem from a physical world to a virtual world. Some organizations may be comfortable with loosened security for their virtual environments, but most will want the same level of security in the virtual environment that they have in the physical environments, which means enforcing least privilege in the virtual world as well as the physical world.

Removing administrator privileges from accounts on virtual machines is still a critical part of an organizations security posture. If organizations wish to virtualize applications or desktops, and the users still need to perform administrative tasks or run applications that require administrative rights in the virtual environment, then the user will need to be logging in as an administrator. This means that the virtual environment is still the subject of the same security issues as when they are logged in to a physical machine.

Virtualized Desktop Infrastructure (VDI) environments, such as Citrix, require users to run as administrators to access applications and install associated DLLs. Malware and hackers can exploit these administrative privileges. Additionally, they allow users to:

- Change standard desktop configuration settings
- Install unlicensed software and disable security settings

Similarly, in Microsoft or VMware environments, users with administrative access often inadvertently delete printers for other users, causing disruption in business and creating unnecessary helpdesk overhead.

According to Gartner, VDI adoption is growing at a rapid rate. By 2013, it is expected that more than 40%of the worldwide professional PC market and 70%of organizations will have adopted PC application virtualization. Because of privilege requirements associated with application delivery, customers are forced to run their users as administrators in VDI environments. Since the desktop application support cost reduction, Forrester estimates of 80% are compelling; customers accept the relaxed security posture, opening themselves up to risks from accidental, intentional, and indirect misuse of privilege.

Attaining least privilege user posture in virtualized desktop environments is challenging and customers are consistently forced to make compromises on security in favor of cost-savings.

Desktop Registry and File System Virtualization

In Windows Vista, Microsoft introduced Registry and File System Virtualization to solve some of the problems with application compatibility. Some applications require full access to certain areas of the operating system that are off limits to standard users. These applications might try to write data to the "Program Files" directory or the "HKEY_LOCAL_MACHINE" hive of the registry, for example. Standard users do not have permission to write to these areas of the file system and registry, so when a user launches an application on Windows XP that needs access to these locations, they would eventually see an error when the application tries to access data stored in these locations.

In Windows Vista and Windows 7, Microsoft has redirected the access to these locations to a virtual store in an area of the operating system that the user has access to. This attempt to solve the problem of application compatibility for applications that need rights to areas of the file system or registry that are off limits to a standard user introduces several problems. One example is that applications may not be compatible with each other.

For example, if an application has written data to a virtual store, another application that needs access to the data in the virtual store will not be able to access it. A similar problem occurs when an application stores data in a virtual store and multiple users of the same machine need access to it. A simplified example of this would be a game that stores its high score file in the "Program Files" directory. With file system virtualization, the high-score file would be stored in the user's profile, instead of Program Files, and thus any subsequent player would store a copy of the high score in their profile. This means that every user of the machine would have the high score! Imagine how this might impact line-of-business applications that multiple people use on the same machine.

Another issue with registry and file system virtualization is the fact that it can cause significant confusion for end users. If an end user has traditionally stored files in a directory that will be virtualized in Windows 7, the user will not know where to go to get the files if they need to copy, view, or e-mail them because the files will no longer be where the end user intended on storing them; they will actually be in the virtual store in the user's profile.

Reads and writes to the following location:
C:\Program Files (x86)\My Application A

Would be redirected to the virtual store:
C:\Users\%username%\AppData\Local\VirtualStore\Program Files
(x86)\My Application A

All subsequent access for that specific application would be redirected to
this location as well; however, other applications that need access to this
data will not know where to go to get it because it has been virtualized.

The Virtual Shell Game

Ever have a magician or street performer get you to bet on the shell game?
You know the game, the one where something is hidden under one of three
shells and then they move the shells quickly while you try to keep track of
where you think the object is. You can never win this game because the object is never where you think it is courtesy of some incredible sleight of
hand. Turns out this is the game that can happen when administrators of
virtualized environments don't always set the permissions and/or policies
correctly. As stated previously, you may think that everyone can see (or has
permission to view/edit) some particular file or application, when in fact
only the admin or a subset of users can. This challenge gets blown into huge
proportions courtesy of the ease at which new virtual environments can be
launched by the administrator with hypervisor access.

Commonly called "virtual sprawl," this can become the electronic version of
the shell game when good people either intentionally want to hide something or accidently misplace key data or applications. Virtual administrators
are like the physical server administrators described in the last chapter, but
with the ability to do things without necessarily needing more hardware,
greatly reducing the typical lags that may result in better planning. It seems
that every organization we talk to nowadays is undergoing huge shifts to virtual or cloud-based computing all in the name of green computing, reducing
IT capital and operational expenses. Unfortunately, this is also giving rise to
a different type of potential insider threat.

Controlling Virtual Sprawl with Least Privilege

Virtual sprawl is the new plague of IT (Figure 6-2). You know a problem has
achieved mainstream status when such headlines as "Virtual Sprawl Hits
Wall Street" appear.

New applications have made it so easy to create virtualized environments on existing platforms that it seems one crops up every time a line of business manager requests a new resource. If you thought server sprawl was bad, just look at what can happen in a virtualized environment.

It usually doesn't matter what the corporate policy, governance, or regulatory requirements implications are to the administrator creating that new environment; however, the implications to the CSO or anyone looking to satisfy audits are potentially huge.

Without proper controls, administrators with full access to the hypervisor can intentionally, accidentally, or indirectly misuse privilege and cause harm.

So how can an organization protect itself from virtual sprawl?

The easy answer is *don't allow it*. But that is a lot harder to enforce than to say. According to David Lynch in the *Virtualization Journal*, "Virtual Sprawl is not the problem. The real solution is to attack the cause as well as the symptom." A key "cause" is the unregulated administration of the hypervisor. Without policy-based controls, an administrator of your virtual environment has carte blanche to do as they please. Implementing a PIM solution will ensure a least privilege environment whereby the admin will only be able to do what policy dictates and the embedded logging will facilitate any audit and remediation as required.

In addition to virtual sprawl, a PIM solution correctly implemented can also eliminate other potential harms caused by misuse of privilege in virtualized environments.

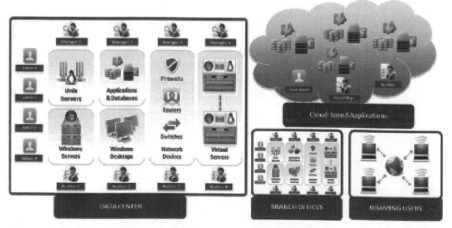

Figure 6-2. Architecture of the cloud

Top Ten Reasons to Implement Least Privilege for Virtualized Servers

Taking a more tongue-in-cheek approach to highlighting the types of privilege misuse that occurs daily on virtual servers inside most organizations, we thought that a top-ten list approach might appeal to you as well. How many of these have you seen throughout your organization?

#10—Sam, the CSO, can now sleep nights knowing that excess privileges in virtualized environments will no longer be responsible for failing a SOX, HIPAA, PCI, DSS, GLBA, or FDCC and FISMA audit (even though he isn't required to even deal with the last two).

#9—Andy the Auditor can get a full report of who has what entitlements, even across virtualized environments, to instantly satisfy compliance successfully instead of taking weeks of manual effort.

#8—Ted in Tech Support won't be able to reset file and directory permissions on any virtual server he has admin rights to so liberally that anyone with a login can access confidential data just because it makes his job easier.

#7—Sid in Development won't be able to download Apache applications or any other unauthorized open source "tools" and potentially inject malware into our corporate network because he was able to commandeer his own virtual server admin credentials.

#6—Fiona and Felix, our new VMware administrators, won't keep making the same View Composer enablement mistake.

#5—Vito, the ever-industrious programmer and closet gamer, will not be able to run Runescape bots on our corporate virtual servers.

#4—Alice, our outsourced VM support engineer, will no longer be responsible for DNS misconfiguration errors as her role won't facilitate this level of admin privilege.

#3—Fred in IT won't be able to steal company data from our virtual servers like that Goldman programmer and sell it to a competitor for $1M.

#2—Sarah, the CIO, will no longer have to fear that virtual sprawl will be the next topic for a board review because policies weren't enforced at the hypervisor admin level.

#1—Tony, the Palo Alto VMware administrator, will no longer be able clone virtual servers with sensitive data and then delete and remount them to bypass security and steal company secrets.

Role-Based Access Control

One of the most challenging problems when managing large networks, virtual or physical, comes from the high costs and complexities of IT security administration. To help counteract these threats, the conception of Role-Based Access Control (RBAC) began focusing around multi-user and multi-application online systems that were pioneered in the 1970s. The essential notion of RBAC is establishing permissions based on the functional roles within the enterprise, and then applying a spotlight on aptly assigning users to a role or set of roles.

RBAC has evolved into a dominant blueprint for advanced access control mainly because the end goal is to reduce the complexity and cost of security administration for large or small networked applications. From theoretical inception to the present practical interpretation, most IT vendors have incorporated RBAC, in some form or fashion, and technology is finding applications in a broad spectrum of industries, ranging from healthcare to defense, in addition to the mainstream commerce systems for which it was designed.

Vendors have incorporated RBAC features into their database, system management, and operating system products. Ironically, while there has been a growing global market for a product solution to infuse an RBAC concept into reality, every vendor's products have been independently developed without any attempt at standardizing salient RBAC features.

As a result, RBAC is seen as an amorphous concept interpreted in different ways by various researchers, organizations, and system developers ranging from simple to elaborate and sophisticated RBAC models. Without standardized models that can be applied and understood between organizations, it becomes more apparent that these products may never provide the true reduction in cost and complexity that RBAC was originally intended to solve.

After acknowledging the problematic circumstances that could be achieved due to no RBAC regularity, the National Institute of Standards and Technology (NIST) produced the NIST RBAC model to provide a blueprint of standardization over a core set of RBAC features.

The benefits of this undertaking include a common set of benchmarks for vendors already developing RBAC mechanisms to implement into their enterprise operations. It will also give IT consumers, the principal beneficiaries of RBAC technology, a basis for creating uniform acquisition specifications.

Each RBAC implementation varies in its capabilities and method of management. In a multi-platform environment, these differences introduce higher administration hours and costs because the various RBAC models are not consistent in administration and operation methodology. The differences among these implementations also increase the potential for misconfiguration and related security issues. Lastly, most vendors' RBAC solutions are to some extent "host-centric." Meaning maintenance operations may have to be performed on each host.

RBAC Is Not the Same as ACLs

RBAC differs from access control lists (ACLs) used in traditional discretionary access control systems in that it assigns permissions to specific operations with meaning in the organization rather than to low-level data objects. For example, an ACL could be used to grant or deny "write access" to a particular system file, but it would not dictate how that file could be changed.

In an RBAC-based model, an operation might be to create a "credit account" transaction in a financial application or to populate a "blood-sugar level test" record in a medical application. The assignment of specific permissions to perform a particular operation is beneficial, because the operations are granular in meaning within the application.

RBAC has been shown to be particularly well-suited to separation-of-duties requirements, which ensure that two or more people must be involved in authorizing critical operations. Necessary and sufficient conditions for safety of separation of duties in RBAC have been analyzed.

An underlying principle of separation of duties is that no individual should be able to affect a breach of security through dual privilege. By extension, no person may hold a role that exercises audit, control, or review authority over another concurrently held role.

Too Much Trust?

In a *Computerworld* article from November 2010, exploring the "scary side of virtualization," the reporter took some time out in a sidebar to offer some sage staffing advice.

His riposte, "Beware the All-Powerful Admin," made clear the risk of giving server admins the "keys to the kingdom"—not a good thing, so consultants and IT execs unanimously agree.

They might, for example, create virtual FTP servers "or they may inadvertently use a virtual-machine migration tool to move a server onto different hardware for maintenance reasons, without realizing that the new host is on an untrusted network segment."

His sage advice is to establish a clear separation of duties in virtual infrastructures, and develop a strong change-management process that includes issuing change-management tickets.

We naturally would agree, but with one caveat. Businesses don't rely on trust alone. We also don't invite businesses to put their faith in some kind of metaphysical state that transcends our human frailties, we simply invite you to recognize that people can and do make mistakes, and when they are people with the "keys to the kingdom," these mistakes can be costly.

Better to trust your people and take out an insurance policy against human frailties, whether those be fat-fingered mistakes, or willful misuse of responsibility. In any environment, especially the deployment of virtualized environments, strong identity management practices, and specifically control around privileged access, must be put in place. As the number of virtual hosts increases, there is a natural tendency to create islands of identity that are difficult to manage. As individual virtual servers are created that serve the needs of departmental applications, there will typically be a push from the departments for them to own the access to the server, specifically the privileged access, in the name of departmental efficiency. As the number of identity sources increases, the prospect for orphaned or inappropriate privileged access increases. Without a well-orchestrated management scheme for identity management and privileged access, the company will soon lose control, compromising security and audit compliance.

Least Privilege Architecturally Defined for Virtualized Environments

It is not enough to implement a least privilege solution to managing the physical server that houses a virtualized environment; you will also need to ensure each virtual server is individually protected as well.

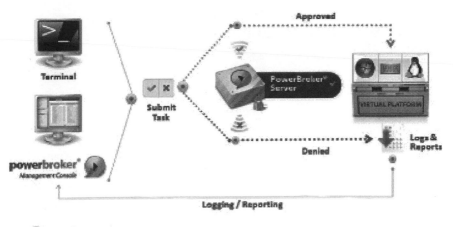

Figure 6-3. Virtual platform

Virtualized Least Privilege Value

A least privilege solution put in place specifically for virtualized environments (Figure 6-3) enables organizations that move to virtualized platforms to control administrative access to the hypervisor/VMM layer while still realizing all virtualization cost efficiencies. Features include:

- Granular delegation of administrative privileges
- Detailed and flexible reporting, including keystroke logging of admin activities
- Two-click entitlement reports
- Programmable role-constrain mechanisms for segregation of duties
- Secure virtual guest and host hypervisors
- Heterogeneous virtualization platforms such as VMware ESX, Solaris Zones, AIX WPAR, and IBM z/VM

Weighing-In

Virtualization has been, and will continue to be, not just a buzzword but a very real and viable approach for lowering costs in the IT sector. As technology advances, more and more companies will move their assets into this space. We've discussed how important it is to protect assets in the virtual world, and we've brought to light the reasons this protection is necessary.

The bottom line is this—least privilege is absolutely necessary for all machines, whether they are physical or virtual.

Let's hear thoughts from our Insider Heroes:

Secure Sam:

Gone are the days where privileges don't need to be managed. We live in a world where data is being stolen on a daily basis, and it is every company's responsibility to secure their mission-critical information. The last thing I want is for a virtual environment within my organization to be out of control. A lot of things can make virtual assets difficult to manage—poorly delegated hypervisor rights, virtual sprawl as a result of bad planning, and too many contributors to guest and host systems. What it comes down to, for my company at least, is this—policies. Policies need to be enforced both for the hypervisor and at the hypervisor level. Just as with physical resources, the virtual ones need to be protected in the same ways. Least privilege is necessary for both security and compliance, and it is especially critical for those assets housed in the clouds and being accessed on virtual platforms.

Least Privilege Lucy:

Managing a network is a challenging task, and one that comes with both high risks and significant costs. This becomes especially true in a virtual environment, where privileges must be administered at the most granular level. In this chapter, we discussed RBAC, which sets permissions based on job descriptions within any given company. This concept is the basis of the least privilege model, and is paramount in the protection of any resources that may have been made virtual. Any desktops, applications, or servers that are taken to the cloud versus being physical still need the exact same protections regular machines do. The most important thing in my mind is to have a very distinct and clear separation of duties in virtual infrastructures. It's so important to have these types of policies in place—it makes security a reality in organizations.

Compliance Carl:

One of the most interesting statements I hear from various companies I audit is that "we went virtual, so we're compliant." I think there are a lot of misconceptions around virtualization, but one that needs to be corrected immediately is that going virtual takes away non-compliance threats. It absolutely does not. If anything, it adds more risks. As was talked about earlier, granular management of privileged users is necessary for the security of physical machines, but it's even more important to the protection of virtualized resources. When you think about it, a virtual asset is susceptible to far more threats because so many administrative privileges are unmanaged in that environment. A least privilege solution is vital in this case—it provides granular identity management on both guest operating systems as well as to hypervisor hosts. Without confining users to only that data they need for job function, the virtualized environment will not be secure. Granular management of privileges is the only way for companies' sensitive information to remain compliant in the cloud.

Secure Multi-Tenancy for Private, Public, and Hybrid Clouds

"As organizations adopt cloud services, the human element takes on an even more profound importance. It is critical therefore that consumers of cloud services understand what providers are doing to detect and defend against the malicious insider threat."

—Cloud Security Alliance, Top Threats to Cloud Computing V1.0

It seems as if every business and IT executive that we talk to lately literally has their "head in the clouds." Every conversation about current or impending strategies for information assets almost universally contains some mention of a public, private, or hybrid cloud deployment. A more interesting observation of these conversations is that the lure of liberating ourselves from the burden of managing applications and data shouldn't mean we stop having high expectations about how those applications and data *are* managed.

If you want to use the public cloud and need to do it in a secure and compliant way, it's a matter of shared responsibility. If you want your cloud vendors to be secure enough to protect your corporation's most sensitive data, then you have to insist on it, and communicate your requirements and oversee the controls. That leaves the final piece of the cloud security puzzle—the often ignored or misunderstood case of the privileged users in the cloud. The cloud is no different from any other domain that requires authorized access. Where there are privileged users, you also need least privilege in order to mitigate the insider threats we have discussed at length throughout this book.

All Clouds Are Not Created Equal

It goes without saying that operating in the cloud is the latest trend in the technology world, and as is the case with every emerging technology, the playing field is not yet clearly defined; "cloud computing" can mean different things to different people.

To some, it is a way of describing commercial services available over the Internet in real-time from outsourced storage and computing capacity to software as a service (SaaS). To others, it is an architecture and set of technologies that facilitate real-time access to information and applications from anywhere via the Internet. Cloud deployments can take three primary approaches:

- *Public Cloud:* This is a computing model whereby a service provider outside of your enterprise will provide the infrastructure and associated management of specific IT resources, usually computing and storage but can also extend to applications and specific information-related services. The primary value is one of "pay for usage" and the ease of access since everything is available via the Internet. It is known and accepted that in most cases, multiple companies are sharing the same physical resources owned and managed by the public cloud vendor but are partitioned into logical or virtual servers for protection across company boundaries.

- *Private Cloud:* Also called corporate cloud or internal cloud, this is really just a new name for an architecture and set of solutions that have already been deployed throughout your enterprise for years. In this computing model, all of the infrastructure and management is physically inside your enterprise, but all of the access is in real-time via the Internet instead of distributed to local desktops or servers.

- *Hybrid Cloud:* Taking advantage of the best of both the public and private cloud architectures is an emerging concept called the hybrid cloud. In this model, some of the infrastructure and services are provided by outside vendors and are linked to infrastructure and services managed inside the physical enterprise, but the ultimate user is oblivious to what is going on "behind the curtain" of their data and application access.

Whether it's the private or public or somewhere in between (hybrid) cloud, it's where we are heading. Just because information and applications are available in such a convenient way does not mean that boundaries should be let down to make all things convenient. The principle of least privilege applies here more than ever before.

The Elusive Unicorn

The ultimate question of security in the cloud revolves around whether or not multiple tenants can coexist without one having any access to the other's data or applications. Truly guaranteed, secure multi-tenancy has been labeled as both somewhat unattainable and the basis by which every cloud vendor's security should be measured. What's interesting about the secure multi-tenancy discussion is that it isn't exclusive to separate companies sharing the same public cloud infrastructure. It turns out that this is as big an issue for private cloud implementations where cross division or department privacy is required either for governance or compliance reason.

Why is secure multi-tenancy in the cloud the elusive unicorn? The short answer centers on the observation that the cloud's greatest strength is also potentially its greatest weakness. Sharing under-utilized resources and paying on a metered or "as-used" basis is a fantastic way to leverage existing investments, control costs, and handle the natural ebbs and flows in capacity planning that usually plagues IT. The challenge comes in when two different organizations with different compliance and security policies are sharing the same resource. How does the cloud provider, even internally for private clouds, ensure that nothing spills from one virtual environment into the other on the physical intersection point, the server?

The sheen of sophistication, the wow factor of something new, dazzles our senses somewhat, and subsequently we invest way too much faith in something—we not only put the cart before the horse, we turn it into a hand cart that we think we can push ourselves. Again we see how human nature is the weak link.

According to Gartner, the private cloud will be introduced primarily as a new way to interface with customers (a self-service catalog of standard services), and a new way to deliver services (automated, giving the user the choice on when to use the service and how much)—it requires a fundamental change in the relationship between business and IT, and the way they do business together. Unlike virtualization, the private cloud must be preceded by changes in organization, processes and business models. It starts with a shift in focus from technologies (servers, virtual machines [VMs] and storage capacity) to services (see "Getting Started With Private Cloud: Services First"). With all these changes, the ultimate question that keeps coming up is "How possible is secure multi-tenancy in public and private cloud environments?"

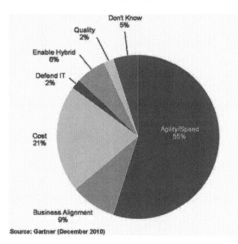

Figure 7-1. Cloud challenges and issues

While cloud computing removes the traditional application silos within the data center and introduces a new level of flexibility and scalability to the IT organization, the support for multi-tenancy computing environments also introduces additional security risks, the most insidious of which is data theft.

The administrative tools used to access the hypervisor/VMM layer a cloud vendor manages must be tightly controlled to maintain a strong security posture. Organizations need to carefully analyze business and security requirements, and must evaluate the depth and reliability of security features and cloud service levels. A privileged identity management (PIM) solution is the only tool that can limit these administrators to specific policy-driven actions as well as provide the granular audit trail to determine actions if remediation is required delivering on the promise of a "more secure" multitenant cloud environment.

Top Ten Reasons to Implement Least Privilege For Private, Public & Hybrid Clouds

Taking a more tongue-in-cheek approach to highlighting the types of privilege misuse that occurs daily in cloud environments, we thought that a top-ten list approach might appeal to you as well. How many of these have you seen throughout your organization?

#10—Andy, the admin at *<insert your public cloud provider name here>*, won't be able to use his admin privileges to your instantiation of a public cloud for data theft.

#9—Clara, your server admin, can't instantiate a new server used for private cloud applications that will facilitate one business unit admin from poking in on the data from other business units' instantiation of a cloud app on the same server.

#8—Sid in development won't be able to code in a back door for privileged access to your hybrid cloud architecture.

#7—Harry, the industrious business unit admin, won't be able to ""tune" your private cloud to what he read was "optimal" on Seth Grodin's latest blog.

#6—Ted in Tech Support won't be able to change cloud file permissions without the proper policy-driven permissions just because it made his job easier today.

#5—Barney, the new business unit manager, won't be able to blame "mistaken identity" for missing his quarterly goal because he read that was something that happens when cloud security goes bad.

#4—Sam, the CSO, won't continue to lose sleep at night fretting over who can hijack admin privileges for any public, private, or hybrid instantiation of their corporate infrastructure.

#3—John, the CEO, won't get called out in the press for a data breach after moving all data to what he thought was a secure, lower-cost private and hybrid cloud.

#2—Vito, a member of the hacker's guild, won't be able to take advantage of the cloud streamlining the efficiency of identity theft.

#1—Bill, the chairman of the board, won't have to explain why he needs to spend $1 million to fix a cloud data breach problem with the statement "at least it's not as much as Sony had to spend for its breach."

Is the Cloud Inherently Secure or Insecure?

The report by the Ponemon Institute in March 2011 on the *Security of Cloud Computing Providers* offered what appear to be some surprising results. According to the study, "the majority of cloud computing providers do not consider security as one of their most important responsibilities."

Given that most studies show security as one of the primary barriers to cloud adoption, this is indeed disappointing news and one might conclude that it's going to be a long time until clouds are appropriate for running enterprise applications. But let's look a little deeper into the data.

The survey was based on responses from 103 providers, so it's a pretty diverse group covering SAAS, PAAS, and IAAS. Many of these cloud providers may be targeting such applications as hosting a blog where security isn't a top priority. In fact, the survey showed that providers believe most of their customers are looking for reduced cost, faster deployment, and improved customer service when they use clouds.

And the study didn't say that cloud providers don't think security is important, but that "the respondents overwhelmingly believe it is the responsibility of the users of cloud computing to ensure the security of the resources they provide." On the other hand, "only 35% of users believe they are most responsible for ensuring security."

So to get the level of security needed to run enterprise applications, we need to clear up the confusion about who should do what.

Who's in Charge of Cloud Security?

Usually, the way we define and implement security is driven by compliance. But despite a wide number of frameworks from the Information Systems Audit and Control Association's (ISACA) Control Objectives for Information and related Technology (COBIT) to Payment Card Industry Data Security Standards (PCI DSS), those compliance standards aren't very clear, leaving ample room for every auditor to interpret them differently.

When you dive deeper into the Ponemon study data, it shows that "cloud providers are most confident about their ability to ensure recovery from significant IT failures and ensure the physical location of data assets are in secure environments." These are two areas where best practices and the compliance standards are well-defined.

On the other hand, cloud providers are "least confident in their ability to restrict privileged user access to sensitive data." At least part of that lack of confidence can surely be attributed to the lack of a clear definition of privileged access and what the appropriate controls are. Since many of the privileged users of a cloud system are the customer's employees, it makes sense that this has got to be an area of shared responsibility between the cloud vendor and the customer. But who should do what and, ultimately, who's in charge?

To the Cloud, or Not

While we can debate the relative security of clouds versus most corporate data centers, there is one area where using a cloud vendor will always represent greater risk—the threat posed by insiders with administrative privileges. We have to quote the Ponemon Institute study that cloud providers are "least confident in their ability to restrict privileged user access to sensitive data."

Now part of that lack of confidence is because their customers control privileged access to the operating system of whatever is running in a cloud-computing environment. So as a customer, you need to take control of that part of the cloud environment and, as many of your peers are doing, use the same tools they do in their data centers to protect privileged account credentials. An effective least privilege solution can be configured to run in a public cloud or in a hybrid mode as an extension of the system in your data center.

That leaves the cloud providers privileged users who administer their hypervisor and control plane environments. Encryption of data is a vital protection and can address a number of concerns about malicious insiders particularly with unstructured data. Database encryption in the cloud is tricky and requires a well-thought-out architecture and key management system.

We don't know of any confirmed breaches by cloud insiders, but that doesn't mean there isn't risk. Most customers don't have deep insight into their cloud provider's technology stacks and operating procedures. So ask them! Some recommendations to become better informed and thus better protected include:

- Review their SAS 70 certifications
- Agree on standards and audit them
- Go onsite and check their controls and look at their logs

Once you make your needs known, we think you will quickly see which cloud providers understand the enterprise customer and want to deliver the security required. In the meantime, *caveat emptor*.

Security in Public Clouds

As stated earlier, you need to take ownership and responsibility for overseeing and requiring compliance and security policies of your chosen cloud vendors. But, how can you do this effectively?

The National Institute of Standards and Technology (NIST), part of the US Department of Commerce, published their *Guidelines on Security and Privacy in Public Cloud Computing* in January 2011. This 60-page report can be best summarized by the quote "accountability for security and privacy in public clouds remains with the organization," a blatant statement of the obvious if we've ever heard one. The report expands on this thought by stating, "assessing and managing risk in cloud computing systems can be a challenge. Throughout the system lifecycle, risks that are identified must be carefully balanced against the security and privacy controls available and the expected benefits from their utilization. Too many controls can be inefficient and ineffective, if the benefits outweigh the costs and associated risks."

John Storts, a blogger over at IT Business Edge, wrote in January 2011 that "cloud service providers, generally, are unaware of the specific security and privacy needs of an organization"—Yes! Ding, ding, ding! And this particular blog goes on to say "so it's wise to have these needs explicitly documented before engaging with them."

We've covered how security is the top issue related to the cloud according to numerous surveys and reports, yet only 23% of cloud customers require proof of compliance from their cloud vendors and only 20% of organizations regularly involve the security team in their cloud choices. With cloud security being such an issue, why aren't we doing more about it?

Organizations that outsource to a cloud vendor seem to make their choices based on price, instead of security. Often this transition involves multiplying the number of IT admins with access to the company's data several-fold and without proper admin controls. So ask your cloud vendor! Ask them how many admins will have access to your data and what policies are in place to protect it. We stated this time and again throughout this book: "trust alone" is not a proper security measure. When human nature is involved at the intersection of technology, whether it is physical, virtual, or cloud-based, you need to take into consideration the obvious uncertainty principle.

Trusted Digital Identities

The US Commerce Department, which just launched an initiative to help create more trusted digital identities. Details were in short supply and there is lots of skepticism and questions about the role of government in any sort of national ID program.

But what is important is that the Commerce Department initiative embraces a model that allows companies to ""pull credentials" when required from a centralized policy-managed repository instead of relying on individual credentials being "pushed" by the user. According to Bob Blakley, Vice President & Distinguished Analyst at Gartner, "we see this public identity infrastructure approach as central to a new emerging architecture where vendors compete in market for identities that provides high-quality identities at lower cost and enterprises focus their Identify and Access Management efforts on developing governance policies that determine what sources of identities are appropriate for their different business processes."

"While Gartner doesn't see these consumer repositories replacing Active Directory anytime soon, and we wouldn't bet on this or any model until it has market traction, in a more diverse world of SaaS, public, private, and hybrid clouds, companies need to anticipate the changes this new model will require in the identity management infrastructure, policies, and controls," states Blakley.

Public Clouds Need Least Privilege

If you want to use the cloud and need to do it in a secure and compliant way, you're going to need to think about who is responsible for what. As numerous studies and articles have highlighted, most cloud vendors today don't provide a platform that's fully up to enterprise security standards.

Cloud vendors need to do their part by providing a good foundation of such security technologies as firewalls, anti-virus and anti-malware, encryption of data in motion, patch management, and log management. Cloud customers also need to do their part by using this foundation to secure their operations and ensure the proper policies and procedures are in place. So that leaves the complicated stuff—shared responsibilities and the special case of the privileged users in the cloud.

Vendor priorities will be aligned with those of their customers. Today for most cloud users those priorities are reducing cost, workload, and deployment time while providing new levels of scalability. Some of these priorities are at odds with the time and resources required to do proper security.

However, if customers demand it and show they will pay for it; vendors will step up and provide the security that's needed. As a recent report by the Ponemon Institute on the *Security of Cloud Computing Providers* showed, "while security as a true service from the cloud is rarely offered to customers today, about one-third of cloud providers in our study are considering such solutions as a new source of revenue sometime in the next two years."

Many cloud vendors have large-scale operations that offer the potential for more resources and expertise to protect your data. But that potential will only be fully realized if customers provide the oversight, funds, and service-level requirements to make sound security processes a good business decision for the vendors. This entails security teams getting more involved, companies allowing security to influence buying decisions, and insisting on regular reporting on security processes and service-level agreements.

If you want your cloud vendors to be secure enough to protect your corporation's most sensitive data, then you have to insist on it, communicate your requirements, oversee the controls, ask for reports, and ultimately take shared responsibility for the security of the cloud. If your cloud provider doesn't implement least privilege within their infrastructure, then you can still protect yourself by implementing that portion on your premise.

A Rose by Any Other Name

When Shakespeare wrote this line in *Romeo and Juliet*, it set the benchmark for quotes representing that what really matters is what something is and not what something is called. So, we find it kind of fun when we hear talk of private clouds representing it as a new and bold IT initiative. As stated earlier, a private cloud is really just a new marketing label for a set of technologies and an architecture that was marketed as "network computing" in the 1980s, "portals" in the 1990s, and "intranets/extranets" at the turn of the millennium.

So, even though private clouds are really just a "marketing wash" of existing concepts, that doesn't mean it shouldn't be any less important to you and your strategy for deployment and management of enterprise information assets. Sometimes it takes good marketing to actually get a smart technical concept more widely accepted across the enterprise, especially by the usually technically illiterate business and finance types who can control the ultimate success or failure of specific IT solutions.

Case Study: Secure Multi-Tenancy in a Private Cloud

A very large multinational bank decided strategically to move to a cloud infrastructure globally for governance and cost reasons in late 2010. In evaluating specific business unit requirements, the lead IT executives discovered concerns regarding confidentiality, security, and the ability to prove compliance.

The complications arose in the uncovering of how difficult it was to segregate the private cloud infrastructure (built on VMware) by business unit while ensuring authorization levels across business units were in line with specific compliance mandates. Each business unit had specific privacy concerns regarding cross-department information access as well as unique compliance reporting requirements. IT needed to manage the authorizations based on corporate-level governance mandates and had their own level of compliance reporting requirements.

Ultimately, a decision was made to make a least privilege solution a mandatory requirement as part of their private cloud stack. In this way, they were able to realize:

- Unified protection from host to guest operating systems.
- Centrally governed privilege delegation for guest VMs.
- Centrally governed privilege delegation for ESX hypervisors.
- Discrete business units could produce compliance reports that included logging and auditing down to the keystroke level.

- Discrete business units could also interrogate event data for ad-hoc drill-down validation of Sarbanes-Oxley (SOX), PCI-DSS, and Federal Financial Institutions Examination Council (FFIEC) compliance.

Logs in the Cloud

As you can see from the previous case study, logs are an important part of compliance. The heart of the matter really is: are logs in the cloud any different than traditional logs? A matter raised by Misha Govshteyn, co-founder of Alert Logic and suggested standard for logging that's specifically for the cloud called CloudLog. He discusses how logs in the cloud are the same, but also different—an oxymoron we support.

We've covered how cloud security is the top issue in the cloud, yet few organizations are doing much about it, and how the cloud requires new models for the same security best practices.

Nothing's changed about privileged access, but now you need to extend that to the hypervisor; nothing's changed about setting and enforcing policy, but now you need to do that across cloud vendors; nothing's changed about logs, but now we need to do keystroke logging and log privileged activity across cloud vendors, hypervisors, and organizations.

Part of the reason there's so much insecurity (pardon the pun) about security in the cloud is this idea that we need to start over from scratch; that security needs to be reinvented for the cloud. But in most cases, we just need to extend what was already in place to the cloud and, as much as we can, to our cloud vendors.

So when you start thinking about cloud security and whether the organization is doing everything they should be, just start with this: are we doing everything we used to but in the cloud?

Implementing Least Privilege in the Cloud

Since this architecture contains elements both on-premise and at your cloud provider, special attention needs to be made to the intersection points. Figure 7-2 shows how to implement a least privilege solution where all elements exist in the hosted environment, while the users on-premise are protected by the least privilege policies.

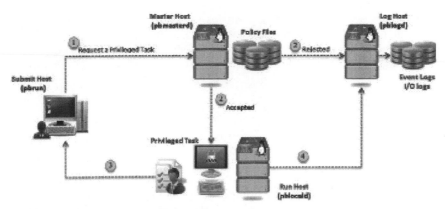

Figure 7-2. Architecture of least privilege

Figure 7-2 shows an example architecture implementing key elements of least privilege on–premise, while still accessing a public cloud infrastructure and using that infrastructure to host the policy files and logs. In this way, you take responsibility for your portion of the security equation.

Weighing In

Establishing least privilege for public, private, and hybrid clouds is necessary to protect the integrity of sensitive information. If the cloud owners and cloud users ensure that PIM solutions are implemented correctly, then the first step to truly secure multi-tenancy has been taken. Without it, insiders could take advantage of the open nature of these environments and the ever-precious data being kept safe could be compromised. Let's hear what our experts have to say

Secure Sam:

One of the strongest arguments for moving data to the cloud is that it re-duces cost, workload, and deployment time. One of the strongest counter arguments is that the time and resources required for properly securing the cloud are often more intensive than the benefits that come from using it. As more and more technology is pointing toward that platform, however, it's obvious that's where we're heading. I think the most important thing to re-alize when discussing this is that a certain degree of governance needs to be in place for an enterprise cloud environment to safely thrive. A lot of that comes from first defining appropriate expectations. Not all users should ex-pect, or be able to access, all information just because it's based in the cloud. Those who need elevated privileges should be granted them, but only if they absolutely need them. The second step is verifying performance. In the cloud more than any other arena, those with privileges need to be monitored. Logs must be kept and records must be analyzed in order for the information in the cloud to be secure. Governance is key.

Least Privilege Lucy:

Least privilege is a concept that applies to all aspects of information technology. It particularly applies to the cloud, as it's the platform with the most access points. In order for a cloud network to be secure to enterprise standards, access must only be granted to users who have the need for it. Most of the time, the environment in a cloud situation has been established with solid technologies—but it's of the utmost importance that users of the platform take responsibility for the information they allow their employees to see. There will always be a need for privileged users—certain applications and commands will always need elevated rights. On the flip side, the entity that houses data for enterprises will always need to be secure. A lot of people get nervous about sending sensitive resources to the cloud, but if it's protected the way physical assets are protected, confidential information will remain just that: confidential. And the way to do that truly is through least privilege. Even if a cloud provider doesn't buy into the concept, it's still something that individual companies can (and should) do within their infrastructures.

Compliance Carl:

As an auditor, I realize most of the security initiatives in organizations are driven by the requirement to be compliant with industry mandates. While one would hope a company is interested in purely protecting its precious assets, compliance does serve as a catalyst for most organizations. And it's a great place to start—there's a reason for regulatory laws regarding data security. The bottom line is simple—they're in place to protect the assets of companies. Once a determination is made to take necessary security measures, that information needs a multi-faceted plan to be successful. Such a plan also needs to include the principle of least privilege. When talking about protecting these resources in the cloud, it's important to emphasize that each user should only have access to the information they absolutely need. In such a public and shared environment, knowing where your data is and who has access to it is paramount to the success of your security strategy. The Ponemon study referenced earlier states that cloud providers are "least confident in their ability to restrict privileged user access to sensitive data." By appropriately managing access to sensitive information, companies can be more confident in the security of their information resources.

Applications, Databases, and Desktop Data Need Least Privilege, Too

"Only 40% of security professionals indicated that existing controls can adequately protect all of their organization's confidential data while the remainder of respondents reported numerous data security gaps."

—Jon Oltsik, Enterprise Strategy Group

Physical, virtual, and cloud infrastructure exists for only one purpose: to store information assets and run applications that give those assets purpose. Since you've kept reading this far, you are now aware of the implications of unmonitored access to this infrastructure, but what about the core reason for buying, implementing and managing all of this in the first place?

All of your investments in legacy applications were done so for specific productivity, profitability, or compete-ability reasons, but the privileges to run them leave gaping security holes. Most applications were originally architected without the concept of granular authorization levels. So how do your users run them today? For most organizations, the answer is to continue to grant full administrative rights so that they don't have to incur the costs of re-architecting and developing those applications without the admin-level requirements.

A better answer, obviously knowing our thoughts on least privilege by now, is not to grant or take away all of those privileges, but to allow users to run them based on what is required for their jobs. This relieves pressure on IT administrators who think the only way out is to upgrade or pay for an in-house patch. This is especially true for database and database-based applications.

Servers Store the Good Stuff…In Databases

In Chapter 5, we spent time discussing how servers are the primary attack point for insider and outside hackers alike. We highlighted that that's because the most important information assets tends to be stored on servers, but what we must point out is the fact that most of that data is residing within a database. Think of it this way—if applications provide the engine to user productivity, the information stored in databases (on servers) and on personal desktops provides the fuel.

So why do databases merit their own chapter?

Put simply, because database-based applications are often also legacy apps. As we have mentioned elsewhere, legacy apps are required for the operation of enterprises everywhere, but the privileges to run them leave gaping security holes in enterprises. The answer, obviously, is not to take away those privileges, but to allow users to run them with a least privilege solution to elevate privileges as required and allowed by policy. This relieves pressure on IT administrators who think the only way out is to completely rewrite code, upgrade to different applications or pay for an in-house patch.

So why not simply upgrade the legacy apps?

As you well know, courtesy of Moore's Law, technology is still getting twice as fast at half the price every 18 months or so, yet businesses still prefer to operate under the assumption pervasive in nearly every enterprise, that "if it isn't broken, don't fix it."

If you won't fix it, then at least be aware that your databases are prone to the same whims of human nature as any other IT environment.

DBA: The Privileged Database User

If you haven't been keeping up with all of the TLA tiles in your organization, then DBA may be one you've missed. DBA stands for database administrator and this is the primary privileged user designated for your database. Like the systems administrator, the DBA has omnipotent access to the database. They can not only monitor and maintain the data, tables, and indexes, but also can add, delete, and modify all of the above to their heart's content.

Similar to your server administrator, the DBA can take on the persona of insider hero Least Privilege Lucy or insider villain Disgruntled Dave, with the only difference being scope of influence limited to the database and not the actual physical or virtual server upon which it resides.

Database Security Risks

As you can imagine, databases are in a class of data storage, organization, and management unto themselves. As such, the inherent security vulnerabilities in which a least privilege solution can help mitigate are also relatively unique. We've uncovered six that should be explored:

1. *Misconfigurations:* Database schemas can be very temperamental and any misconfiguration error can cascade into a huge problem or be so subtle that it may be difficult to uncover the impact. A frequent challenge here is the ambitious developer who somehow gets access to the production system instead of just their development sandbox.

2. *Updates:* Out-of-cycle patching can cause major disruption in operation and potentially lead to lost revenue if done on the primary transaction database. Here is where the ambitious tech support technician or developer believes that blindly trusting that your database vendor's testing capabilities keep current with their latest patch is a good thing.

3. *Application Attacks:* Sometimes the easiest way to attack your database is to attack the outward-facing applications that are connected to that database, especially if those application are web-based. This can also come in the form of database access through non-approved channels such as open source tools capable of bypassing normal admin dashboards.

4. *Transaction Monitoring:* Sometimes it's the smallest of things that can trip you up when looking to satisfy compliance or track down data theft or damage, so monitoring every transaction can be very important. However, it can also drown your data stores in amounts of information too voluminous to even interrogate.

5. *Data Awareness:* What is perceived, or in actuality is, confidential data can be subjective in some organizations and very clearly identified in others. Being aware of what class of data is stored where will be another critical success factor.

6. *Privileged Users:* Our favorite, of course, is the privileged user. As discussed previously, the DBA's omnipotent access to your database must be managed through a least privilege solution in order to ensure your governance and compliance policies are met as well as protect against the misuse of that privilege—intentionally, accidentally, or indirectly.

Legacy Applications Are Still Pervasive

While databases store most anything of value, it's the legacy applications that sit on top of those databases that provide your business users access. Most enterprises have more bespoke legacy applications then they do off-the-shelf software. These applications were mostly written in-house, by developers who more were concerned with making their app work (with admin rights) but without considering the impact granting those rights would have on running other apps. Least privilege is the intersection here between database management, legacy applications, and the infrastructure on which they run.

Your DBAs, IT admins, and business users in each division, department, or business unit will tend to isolate themselves and consider their silo the most important. This again is due to a classic weakness in human nature and the inability to communicate and collaborate between each other. Let's look at the implications of some of these silos.

Desktops Have Legacy Application Challenges as Well

In an enterprise Windows' desktop environment, whether a company has 100 or 10,000 seats, the challenge of managing access is fraught with difficulty. Why? Because every user is going to want to work with their desktop computer the way they work on their own personal computer on their personal time. The proliferation of personal computing has actually made IT's job that much harder as every user considers themselves an expert if they've "Googled" something on the Internet.

One way to control these rogue desktop users is to shut down all privilege. We discussed that at length back in Chapter 4 on desktop least privilege, but then the dreaded UAC pop-up window wreaks havoc with your help desk.

Even if an IT administrator can work out how to circumnavigate Windows User Access Controls or how to set a Group Policy for every application, there will invariably still be a legacy application on which the company relies, which will only run if every user is given administrator status.

In effect, one or more legacy applications force the company to leave the entire network vulnerable to either intentional or accidental damage from giving users a higher level of privileged access than they require.

These applications will have been written in-house, or by a third party provider, to meet the bespoke needs of the company—and yet without recognizing the security risks and compliance headache caused by leaving desktop access wide open.

Equally rife is the use of legacy apps such as Sage Instant Accounts and Intuit QuickBooks, more associated with the individual user or small company, but more often than not used en-masse in larger companies with 100+ desktops.

The impact of these legacy apps is not just the security risks they pose, but also the impact on IT support in fixing the unintentional errors caused by over-privileged desktop users. That's time and money that might be used more strategically, rather than on the tactical day-to-day fire-fighting.

Good role-based user privilege management software can easily circumnavigate the requirement of legacy apps to run desktops on administrator or super user status without requiring their modification or removal.

Desktop DLP Helps Mitigate Different Insider Threats

It may be appropriate to take a small break from a pure least privilege management discussion and highlight another technology that supplements our solution for the mitigation of insider threats on local data stored or accessible by local desktops. Endpoint data leak prevention (DLP) is a solution that compliments the brokering of privilege authorization and aids in securing the perimeter within by dealing with data in use and at rest. DLP leverages a policy engine similar to that of least privilege to ensure specific data is dealt with according to your governance and compliance requirements. Here, specific phrases, paragraphs, or documents can be protected against movement, copy, modification, or deletion.

Loss of customer account details, exposure of confidential information, and theft of sensitive data are typical data leak cases that cost companies up to 5% of revenue every year. Insiders, employees, and contractors who have authorized access to confidential data are liable for 70% of total data leaks.

Compliance Audit Failures

If you can't protect your data in databases, in legacy applications, or on personal desktops, then ultimately you face a compliance audit failure (see Figure 8-1), in addition to potential damage, loss, or theft.

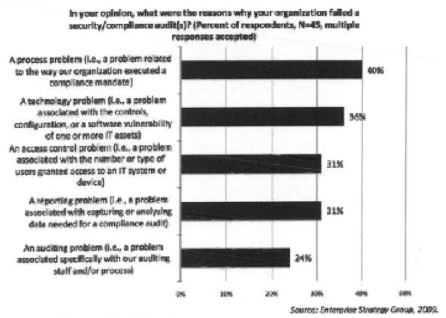

Figure 8-1. Reasons for failed audits

Stolen Fruit

I'm sure you've heard the saying "stolen fruit is the sweetest." It's a phrase that gets thrown around lightly, but it's time to take it to heart. In a day when information and sensitive data are being stolen, manipulated, and blasted for the world to read, this is a saying we all need to look at twice. Hackers, inside security leakers, and thieves all agree: that which is stolen is the sweetest. You don't want to find out how sweet the information in your enterprise will be to them. Steps should to be taken to secure the sensitive information and data in enterprises across the world.

Who are these people stealing the "fruit?" I think you can probably guess— hackers, thieves, and those abusing administrator rights. These are the people enterprises must protect against. According to a study performed by the Professional Association for SQL Server (PASS), 44% of database security challenges come in the form of inside hackers and the abuse of privileges. Outside hackers and thieves do present a threat to the integrity of our databases and the information therein, but our attention should first be turned to those already in our organizations. Often, these individuals have too much access to information they simply do not need. And why do they steal this data? Because your data is truly sweet to them—they see a huge payday without the hard, bitter work. If you think this doesn't apply to you, or that none of your employees are capable of such atrocity, let me turn your attention to the Goldman Sachs debacle. I bet they thought their enterprise wasn't in danger either—yet look at what transpired. How much will the "sweetest fruit" cost your company?

If you are concerned about the security of your enterprise (you should be if you haven't already taken measures to keep your sensitive information safe), it's time to implement a privilege management policy and become compliant with government mandates. It's the only way to prevent the fruits of your company from becoming sweet and stolen. Don't let your employees assign a price to the sweet information in your enterprise. Set up a protocol that allows users just the right amount of access to information.

Top Ten Reasons to Implement Least Privilege for Applications and Databases

Taking a more tongue-in-cheek approach to highlighting the types of privilege misuse that occurs daily in applications and databases inside most organizations, we thought that a top-ten list approach might appeal to you as well. How may of these have you seen throughout your organization?

> #10—Sam, the CSO, can now sleep nights knowing that inappropriate database activities are not only being monitored but also prevented via policy enforcement at a granular level.

> #9—Fiona, the DBA, won't be able to modify the production database instead of the test copy in the sandbox accidentally or even accidentally on purpose.

> #8—Frank, your sole Application Developer, will no longer have to rewrite legacy applications in order to strip out any code requiring administrative privileges.

> #7—Ted, the overzealous Tech Support Tech, won't be able to upgrade your production database to the latest version of Oracle released today before the IT department has had time to vet the impact on current processes and attached applications.

> #6—Ken, the CSO, can delegate database access based on access control policies that leverage external context such as SOX, PCI-DSS, and FFIEC compliance.

#5—Carl, the Compliance Executive, can now quickly identify all privileged users, review entitlements, and if necessary, de-provision obsolete users in order to pass your next enterprise IT audit.

#4—Francine, the COO, can now easily ensure adherence to change control processes across the extended enterprise for all databases and even reconcile with the change ticketing system.

#3—Larry, the new DBA, won't have to call his predecessor, who is now serving eight years in the penitentiary for identity theft and attempted sale of your entire customer credit card transaction database, to learn the new processes for database activity monitoring (DAM).

#2—Beth in Human Resources won't be able to forward the entire company payroll ledger to WikiLeaks because the CEO didn't tell her how great she looked today.

#1—The IT department can still have the 35th annual birthday party next week for that payroll application that requires desktop admin rights, but no one knows where the source code is to make it more contemporary instead of replacing it outright.

In the News

You probably already saw in December of 2010 that a group called Gnosis hacked over one million rows of data from Gawker, claiming the organization had some of the worst security they could have imagined. Gnosis gained access to their database in one day and even Gawker said in an internal memo that they were largely caught unprepared.

Now for your own entertainment, you should see the Wall Street Journal blog of December 13, 2010, which shows that over 3,000 Gawker users had the password "123456" and 2,000 had the password "password". Everyone knows users often set poor passwords when left to their own devices, but the chart presented in the Wall Street Journal blog really brings it to life. Gawker clearly didn't have adequate requirements for more complex passwords.

It's unclear how exactly Gnosis gained access to Gawker's database. They mention that there were a lot of vulnerabilities in outdated software. However, what is clear is their motivation: vengeance, and why Gawker was so easy to hack: lack of preparation.

Vengeance is such a powerful mission that it's created a plethora of music, movies, books, and even video games. In the movie Vengeance, a chef seeks vengeance for a violent attack on his family that left three dead. In real life, vengeance is not always so compelling; Gnosis sought vengeance because they were offended.

Yup, that really is all it takes. Now think back to the last time you fired someone, they quit, or maybe you were the one leaving. How often was the departing employee bitter about something?

Vengeance is easily ignited and when you're a member of the IT team with privileged access to IT systems and special skills, what else would possibly be your weapon of choice? Terry Childs, the former network administrator who was arrested on computer crimes in June 2008 for refusing to divulge the passwords to San Francisco's FiberWAN system, is an example of how IT staff enacts vengeance. Gnosis is how hackers enact vengeance. IT sabotage and penetration is how computer enthusiasts cause damage to those they will it on.

So prepare for it.

Why Give a DAM

The lack of control of privileged database credentials continues to expose corporations to significant risk associated with insecurity and inaccuracy of the key data assets that drive business activities, decisions, and value. We've previously covered the six questions you should ask yourself if you should give a DAM, so now it's time to look a little deeper at the implications.

Specifically, weak control of privilege credentials provides the opportunity for the insiders holding those credentials (or hackers who acquire them) to misuse their elevated privileges to steal or fraudulently manipulate data or simply introduce inaccuracies through human error. The consequences of these unauthorized actions can be severe for businesses, especially if the activity goes undetected for a prolonged period of time. Secondarily, the compliance costs associated with proving to IT audit that adequate database controls around these privileged users are in place is high.

The solutions currently available to corporations today are often times not entirely effective, and are expensive to purchase, deploy, and maintain. Custom-developed solutions that leverage the database's native security and audit features are a common approach. These solutions are expensive to design, develop, maintain, and operate. DAM products on the market today are another alternative. These products provide tools to implement detective and preventative controls for DBAs; however, there are three key weaknesses in these products:

1. The preventative capabilities are driven largely by policies involving rudimentary session attributes, access patterns, and activity thresholds. These do not provide the capability to control activity on a fine-grained basis based on external context.

2. The monitoring capability of many of these products does not provide the level of visibility into what is happening to data assets stored within the database, nor does it provide the activity detail needed to assess impact of the activity and remediate it if necessary.

3. The products are expensive and complex to implement.

DAM Value

First, securing the database is critical. The database is where the business' valuable data assets live, and is therefore most often the target of attack when it comes to frauds and data breaches. Controlling the users that hold elevated privileges on the database is critical to any data security effort. A complete solution to this problem must include the following:

- *Effective Credential Management:* Identifying privileged accounts across database infrastructure. Provisioning access to and privileges on those database systems based on business justification, and quickly de-provisioning access and privilege when justification no longer exists.
- *Policy-Based Access Control and Privilege Delegation:* Control systems based on the principal of least privilege. Privileges are delegated only when needed and authorized (need and authorization based on evaluation of external context such as a change ticketing system), only for the duration to execute distinct authorized change activities.
- *Activity Monitoring and Closed-Loop Reconciliation with Change Management:* Capture, review, and reconcile all activity executed by privileged users against change ticketing to verify that the activity was authorized, followed change-management processes, and did not impact systems or business objectives negatively.
- *Data Audit:* Maintain a forensic audit repository of changes to key data fields, access to key data fields, or change of system configurations and controls that protect those data assets.

- *Compliance Reporting:* Compliance is a by-product of effective controls. A solution must produce evidence that effective control is being maintained.

Implementing Least Privilege for Databases

Fundamentally, the implementation of least privilege for a database isn't that different than implementing least privilege on a server. The difference is that the target is the specific database and associated commands (that is, select, view, copy, delete, etc.) executed by privileged users (DBAs) versus the systems administrator who needs to execute root-level commands.

So, Figure 8-2 should look very familiar to you by now, as it effectively is the same architecture we've presented for physical and virtual servers. Now you are monitoring the DBAs access, enforcing database-specific access policy and DAM instead of the least privilege solution monitoring commands sent to the operating system, enforcing policies, and either elevating the privilege necessary for that command or not along with logging the associated keystrokes and events,.

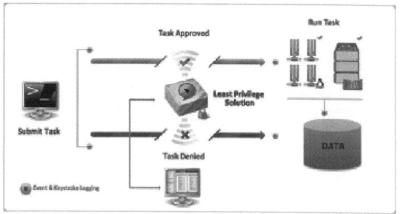

Figure 8-2. Architecture for database least privilege

Controlling Your Privileged Database Users

Implementing a least privilege solution for your databases will also ultimately deliver on the promise of best practices for:

- *Managing privileged credentials:* identifying and managing entitlements

- *Enforcing policy:* establishing and enforcing governance across the extended enterprise
- *Monitoring and reconciling privileged activity:* ensuring that no insider hero turns into an insider villain
- *Maintain a high-quality audit repository:* for business intelligence or remediation purposes
- *Automate compliance reporting:* for speed, ease, and lower costs when time for proving compliance

Weighing In

Least privilege is a critical part in the security of all of a company's assets. By turning first to the insiders with access to databases, applications, and desktop data, organizations can make sure those closest to an enterprise's sensitive information are prevented from leaking or accidentally manipulating it.

Let's hear what our Insider Heroes have to say.

Secure Sam:

Protecting information from insiders is crucial to the security of an enterprise. Obviously, not all insiders are malicious—people make mistakes just as much as they have intentions of pilfering corporate information from secure databases. It's crucial to prevent people within your organization from sabotaging (whether accidentally or on purpose) your sensitive information and this responsibility lies with you. As someone in a position of authority over the IT resources in your enterprise, you must be the one to govern the usage of these assets and the people who access them. Attention should be focused first on the internal structure of security. A handle must first be had on what goes on inside the walls of your individual enterprises, especially since it's how insiders use their privileges that determines how easy it is for outsiders to get in. Don't allow users free access to assets—especially when it comes to applications, databases, and desktops. You must secure procedures to govern the usage of resources in your company. There really is no other way to be compliant and secure.

Least Privilege Lucy:

By now you understand the concept of least privilege. You get why it's important, and you know it's an important step in securing your company's IT infrastructure. Least privilege helps mitigate so many security vulnerabilities that it's unwise to ignore it when making your plan for securing sensitive information. Especially when talking about databases and the data stored therein, companies take a huge risk by not monitoring and managing users' access to such information. The chapter spelled out six of the most susceptible vulnerabilities that least privilege can ease, and I whole-heartedly stand behind them. Too many times I've seen users misconfigure schemas and cause horrendous problems. Updates and application attacks are among the highest offenders, as well. It is so important for enterprises to be aware of the data in their systems, as well as to monitor the usage of said information. Without constantly watching what is moving and how it's moving, you're turning your back on a glaring security problem. The same goes for the individuals who have access to your sensitive data. It's paramount that they (along with their privileges) be monitored tightly.

Compliance Carl:

Compliance isn't only beneficial because it helps you avoid hefty fines. It ensures security of IT resources and stability in information infrastructures. If your company is incapable of protecting its assets, a failed audit is only a matter of time. Unfortunately, that failed audit is the driver behind most companies' security efforts. The deeper issue is damage to database information, loss of resources, or theft. Insiders are a hugely contributing factor to the security of an enterprise's data. All around are reports of breaches—the devastating results of insiders whose privileges haven't been reigned in. There are mandates preventing such breaches... a concept I feel most companies forget. Compliance isn't about paying the government money or having to jump through more hoops to make Uncle Sam happy. Quite the opposite actually; compliance makes your information safe. It's as simple as that. It's also very black and white—either you're following mandates or you're not. One thing I've noticed in various companies is that least privilege is a common denominator to passing audits and following mandates. It's a principle that helps your company be successful with security. Without fail. If a company has implemented a least privilege policy, they will be found compliant. Even better, they will be free from the devastating side effects of letting insiders run free.

Security Does Not Equal Compliance

"Expensive episodic compliance exercises are giving way to continuous cost-sustainable compliance processes."

—Ian Glazer, Gartner Inc.

Analysts know better than any that compliance is not a checklist of policies to create, but instead a benchmark for the better integration of people, technology, and processes. Or at least, that's what compliance rules and regulations should impel businesses to create. The rules and laws of each individual company must be strict and consistent to ensure productivity, compliance, and security. These rules must be constantly monitored and updated by both a human resources (HR) rep that understands rank and privilege and IT administrators who can implement privileges based on the description given by HR.

All too often though, management can mistake well-planned and executed information security architecture with satisfaction of compliance and regulatory statutes. Unfortunately, nothing could be further from the truth. Great, or even good, security practices don't always mean compliance, and vice versa. Satisfying compliance and regulatory mandates to the letter may still leave you vulnerable to security breaches, especially the dreaded insider attack that we have discussed at length throughout this book.

This is another area where the intersection of human nature and technology becomes important and requires least privilege as a key success factor for establishing a compliant architecture. The principle of least privilege was developed more than 30 years ago by the United States Department of Defense (DoD). This principle "requires that each subject in a system be granted the most restrictive set of privileges needed for the performance of authorized tasks. The application of this principle limits the damage that can result from accident, error, or unauthorized use." By eliminating administrator privileges from your environment, you are moving that environment toward one that fulfills this principle's goals. You are at the same time going far toward fulfilling the requirements of most of the current regulations, as almost all have some form of clause emphasizing fraud control and have identified "privileged access" as an area of higher risk by which fraud has been committed.

GRC Demystified

Every discussion around security and compliance brings up yet another acronym that must be dissected, analyzed, and demystified. In this case, the acronym is GRC and is the short form for *governance, risk, and compliance*. These three letters seem to have more events, budget dollars, companies, real and "marketectured" solutions, publications, bloggers, certifications, and water-cooler conversations than any other acronym (with perhaps FUD [fear, uncertainty, and doubt] as the exception, but that is the subject of another book).

Let's look at each of these areas individually for a better understanding of how they fit within your strategy.

Governance

Corporate governance ensures accountability across the extended enterprise. It facilitates staying competitive and satisfying ever-changing government regulations while providing mechanisms and controls to reduce the inefficiencies that arise when individuals misuse privileges granted to them.

If You Can't Change It, You Can't Govern It

A key aspect of corporate governance is ensuring that the changes decided by management are in fact enforced across every office and IT system despite geographic, network, and operating system differences. This can be especially difficult for companies that grow through acquisition where newly acquired IT assets rarely match current corporate standards. Getting new policies rolled out and enforced to new acquisition assets can be extremely time consuming and tedious work but very necessary to maintain compliance. Without these types of controls, companies face the dire consequences already seen by the likes of Enron and MCI (formerly WorldCom). We have already discussed the intentional, accidental, and indirect misuse of privilege at length in all of the previous chapters.

Implementing a privilege identity management (PIM) solution can significantly impact corporate governance accountability and change management in real-time across the extended enterprise, as well as eliminate the misuse of privilege across heterogeneous systems and virtualized, or even cloud-based, administrators. Any change to privileged access can be accomplished from a centralized console and pushed to every environment in real-time. All entitlements and audit logs can also be reviewed on-demand and therefore your company can ensure governance mandates.

Steps to Good Governance

Managing and auditing corporate governance initiatives are an often-overlooked area for executives and IT professionals. Reading any one of the thousands of business books that describe successful companies, you will uncover that It was their ability to react and pro-act to market changes at an enterprise level that allowed them to exceed market or competitive norms. Likewise, in those same books, you will find examples of failed companies whose IT infrastructure actually prevented or inhibited their ability to enforce change across all employees.

Audits for compliance are typically required, but extending this practice to real-time governance can be the difference between success and failure for companies in today's ever-changing market climates.

- Making changes in who has privilege to do what on specific IT resources (servers, desktops, network devices, virtual & cloud environments) should be as simple as making a central policy change and having that propagated and enforced in real-time across the extended enterprise.

- Implementing a PIM solution is the best first step in establishing this real-time corporate governance.

Risk

Risk is a very subjective subject. What is an acceptable level to one executive or company may be considered far too radical for another. We haven't seen anything that can guarantee 100% safety when it comes to IT security, but we have seen some architectures that come close. So, at best, you can only hope to manage risk and the associated expectation around cost of protection versus cost of damage reparation.

At some point in your life, you have probably heard the story about closing the barn doors after the horses have already left the stable and its corollary that "an ounce of prevention is worth a pound of cure." The same can be said for dealing with insider threats and the types of solutions available today.

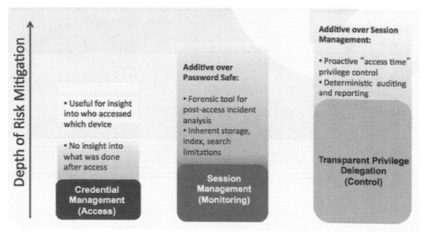

Figure 9-1. Levels of insider threat mitigation solution

Fundamentally, you will find three levels of insider threat mitigation solutions (Figure 9-1) available to you:

- *Credential Management:* Vaulting of passwords and credentials to control who has access to what resources under what circumstances. On the positive side, you will know who was logged into a resource when a breach occurred, but the challenge with this technology is the lack of visibility into what they did once they were logged in. In this situation, you have eliminated users maintaining their own credentials and facilitate the access to IT resources through a web-based shared account password management (SAPM) solution. When the user desires access, they go to a specific web screen that then logs the user into the requested resource based on some recognized stored policy. The good news here is that in the event someone misuses that resource, you have a record of who was using it at the time of the breach. This is the equivalent of knowing who did the damage but not what they did.

- *Session Management:* In addition to managing credentials, some solutions can also log everything done by individuals while logged into a resource. On the positive side, you will know who was there and what they did so that you can possibly remediate the damage, but the challenge with this technology is the inability to prevent the damage from being done in the first place. In this situation, you are building on password management with the addition of automatic logging of every event (or keystroke) to another server of what was done once someone is granted access to the resource. If harm does occur in this situation, then you not only know who did the harm but what they did, so you can "unwind" or fix what was done.

- *Privilege Management:* In addition to managing credentials and logging activities, this solution can also enforce policy at a fine-grained entitlements level to ensure only those with proper authorization can do what they are attempting to do. On the positive side, you not only manage credentials and log transactions, you also prevent damage from occurring by limiting the privileges to only those necessary. In this situation, you are delegating privileges (system authorizations) to specific users based on defined, centralized corporate policy. This builds on session logging and delivers all of the previous value, but now limits the damage potentially done as it limits what authorizations are available based on policy. In effect, you have prevented harm from being done and have a record of who attempted to do harm and what they attempted to do.

Compliance: The Big C

In a survey conducted by Unisphere Research, results showed that even though many DBAs are willing to assume much-needed security practices in their daily duties, there is an overwhelming communication disconnect between these data managers and the security and executive leadership responsible for the data security at the end of the day.

The report surveyed 761 members of the Professional Association for SQL Server (PASS) in September 2010. Behind human error, the most commonly cited challenges to database security are insider hacks and the abuse of privileges (44%).

The key take away from the report is that there is a disconnect between what DBAs know needs to be done at the technical level versus the amount of support and awareness the executives on the business side actually give to them.

Monitoring database access is part of the solution, but addressing the misuse of privilege requires going beyond that. It is just as essential to continually audit privileges to ensure that employees and partners only have access to the minimum amount of sensitive data necessary to perform their duties. This requirement for separation of duties is also a cornerstone of virtually all compliance regulations.

One in five respondents "fears that their organization will experience a major data breach over the coming months, but few are aware of the potential costs to their organizations." Among those respondents that are aware of where data breaches have occurred, they cite "a pattern of inside abuse and errors."

Cloud Compliance Introduces New Issues

One of greatest challenges for organizations leveraging cloud environments is demonstrating policy compliance. For many business functions that commonly run in the cloud, such as hosting web sites and wikis, it is often sufficient to have a cloud provider vouch for the security of the underlying infrastructure. However, for business-critical processes and sensitive data, it is absolutely essential for organizations to be able to verify for themselves that the underlying cloud infrastructure is secure.

The use of virtual machines adds further complexity into the mix, since creating an identity for an individual virtual machine and tracking that virtual machine from creation to deletion can be challenging for even the most mature virtualized environments. Proving that the physical and virtual infrastructure of the cloud can be trusted becomes even more difficult when those infrastructure components are wholly owned and managed by external service providers.

Cloud providers must be able to demonstrate that they have tested and can ensure that privileged user access is controlled and monitored. For instance, ISO/IEC 27001 requires an organization to create an information security management system (ISMS). This enables an organization to use a risk-based approach to identifying and satisfying all compliance requirements, justify the selection and implementation of controls, and provide measurable evidence that the controls are operating effectively.

Organizations that claim to have adopted the ISO 27001 standard can therefore be formally audited and certified compliant with the standard. It is already fairly well known and accepted outside of the US and is slowly gaining awareness and acceptance within the US. ISO 27001 requires that management:

1. Systematically examine the organization's information security risks, taking account of the threats, vulnerabilities, and impacts;

2. Design and implement a coherent and comprehensive suite of information security controls and/or other forms of risk treatment (such as risk avoidance or risk transfer) to address those risks that are deemed unacceptable; and

3. Adopt an overarching management process to ensure that the information security controls continue to meet the organization's information security needs on an ongoing basis.

When appropriate, organizations should also ask for a commitment from providers to meet regulatory standards such as the Payment Card Industry (PCI) Data Security Standard (DSS), Health Insurance Portability and Accountability Act (HIPAA) in the US, and the EU Data Protection Directive.

Alphabet Soup

In the United States alone, there are over 300 federal agencies that have posted tens of thousands of regulations that need to be traversed, understood, and acted upon in order to maintain compliance. The US government has a web site, regulations.gov, that not only lists the regulations but has a dedicated page to list "Regulations with Comment Periods Coming Soon" to make sure you don't miss any reporting deadlines.

Unfortunately, there are more acronyms here than permutations available for uniqueness. So, you need to be careful when someone talks about an acronym in a conversation. For example, when talking about PCI, you need to determine if they are referring to the Payment Card Industry Data Security Standard or Peripheral Component Interconnect standard for hardware expansion bus communication.

Let's look a little closer at some of the more visible regulations that are especially affected by least privilege or the lack thereof. To illustrate, we will do a deep dive on HIPAA to show how details of a regulation can sometimes be a bit tricky, then highlight some of the other regulations to point you in the right direction. There are many other resources available to take you through the details of each and every regulation and we didn't feel this book was the appropriate place for that.

HIPAA

In 1996, the Department of Health & Human Services set the rules for protection of individually identifiable health information under the Health Insurance Portability and Accountability Act (HIPAA).

The majority of HIPAA's requirements that relate to IT systems are contained within section 45 CFR 164, commonly known as "the final rule." This final rule outlines HIPAA's guidance associated with the integrity, availability, and privacy of ePHI. It also outlines guidance associated with authentication to and access control within systems that contain ePHI data, as well as the requirements for auditing such systems. The following list highlights Information about that guidance:

- *Integrity of ePHI Data—45 CFR 164.312(c)(1), (2), & (e)(2)(i)*: Technical controls must be implemented that protect ePHI from improper alteration or destruction until it is disposed.
- *Availability of ePHI Data—45 CFR 164.308(a)(7)(ii)*: Procedures must be established and implemented that create and maintain retrievable and exact copies of ePHI data. Also, procedures must be established and implemented to restore any lost data.
- *Authentication to ePHI Data Systems—45 CFR 164.312(d)*: Systems and/or procedures must be established that verify the person or entity seeking access to ePHI data is the one claimed.
- *Access Control in ePHI Data Systems—45 CFR 164.312(a)(1), (2), & (3)*: Systems that contain ePHI data must allow access only to those persons or software programs that have been granted access rights. Unique IDs must be assigned for identifying and tracking users. Sessions must be terminated when they have become inactive.
- *Audit of ePHI Data Systems—45 CFR 164.308(a)(5)(ii)(c) & 164.312(b)*: Technical controls must be implemented that record and examine the activity in ePHI data systems as well as procedures that monitor logins and report discrepancies.

The widespread distribution of administrator rights in an organization is at direct odds with these requirements. Such is the case because administrator rights enable complete and unrestricted access to an entire system for the specified user. Additionally, with administrator rights, users can alter system records and generally subvert the requirements for tracking users who access information.

So, where do HIPAA, admin rights, and least privilege intersect?

As with other compliance regulations, HIPAA's guidance revolves around the protection of personal data through the implementation of technical controls. The controls also protect that data from corruption or change through established systems that enforce data integrity. IT organizations are also charged with implementing a set of "controls" that restrict the actions of users to just those tasks required by their job roles. Further, when users actually work with business systems, their activities must be monitored and logged into a verifiable database. This task would be easy if it were natively supported by the Windows operating system. Although not explicitly stated, it is generally accepted that a central goal of HIPAA as well as every other industry, governmental, and regulatory compliance statute is the implementation of least privilege.

We discussed at length how least privilege is more than simply eliminating administrator rights. Least privilege can more broadly be described as the intersection of the user's role in the organization, the overarching corporate security policy of that organization, and the tasks that are available to be accomplished within the IT infrastructure. In effect, an environment that fulfills the requirements of least privilege will be very granularly capable of providing access to each person based on their needs.

PCI DSS

Another key regulation is the Payment Card Industry (PCI) Data Security Standard (DSS), which is a set of comprehensive requirements for enhancing payment account data security in an effort to thwart the theft of sensitive cardholder information. The core group of requirements is as follows:

- Build and maintain a secure network
- Protect cardholder data
- Maintain a vulnerability management program
- Implement strong access control measures
- Regularly monitor and test networks;
- Maintain an information security policy

On October 28, 2010, the PCI Security Standards Council (SSC) unveiled version 2.0 of the PCI DSS. Until then, PCI DSS had not had an update since version 1.2 in October 2008. The recent "Summary of Changes" document released by the PCI SSC covers the proposed changes in version 2.0, and as experts expected, few alterations were made between the summary and the final release.

However, one important area to note in the new version is in the PCI DSS Intro and Various Requirements section. In this section, the focus is on virtualization, and though minor, it expands the definition of system components to include virtual components. This addition should alert enterprises to begin assessing their security policies to virtual servers and desktops in their IT environment.

Organizations moving their physical server infrastructure onto virtual platforms for cost savings are finding their virtual hosts and guests are now open to new security and non-compliance risks. Attaining least privilege user posture in virtualized desktop and server environments is challenging and customers are consistently forced to make compromises on security in favor of cost-savings.

Remember, the PCI DSS has never been a compliance program. It is a standard baseline for assessing compliance that the five major card brands (Visa, MasterCard, American Express, Discover, and JCB) agreed to use as the foundation for their actual, individual compliance programs. At the end of the day, each of the five major card brands still retains final say on compliance and can implement their own compliance requirements over and above the PCI DSS (and Payment Application Data Security Standard [PA DSS]) when or if they see fit.

The Cost of SOX Is Declining?

No, we're not talking about socks that protect your feet; we're talking about the government regulation that most of you are worried about. Sarbanes-Oxley (SOX) was enacted in 2002 to counter a number of major corporate and accounting scandals and establish a set of public accounting reforms and investor protection mandates.

Protiviti released a new study in the spring of 2011 on the effectiveness and costs of SOX compliance with a number of interesting insights for IT managers who are concerned about the effectiveness and costs of their IT controls. The overall results are encouraging.

According to Protiviti's 2011 SOX Compliance Survey, the cost of SOX compliance is declining and most participants believe the benefits of the controls outweigh the costs. Now we are little skeptical that all of the companies surveyed are including the full impact of SOX controls on IT costs, especially since less than 50% track and report the hours and costs of compliance. I suspect some companies have just gotten comfortable that some of the activities they added are just part of a new normal. Sort of like the metaphor of a slowly boiling frog not jumping out of the pot.

Nevertheless, the way companies are approaching the continuous improvement in their SOX controls is telling. They are simultaneously reducing costs and increasing the effectiveness and efficiency of operations by following a number of key strategies:

- Using the COSA framework to define best practices. COBIT would provide a similar framework for IT.
- Increase use of automated controls and continuous monitoring including a shift to preventative rather than detective controls.
- Use of data mining and analytics to increase understanding of process performance.
- Consolidating IT processes, platforms, and systems.

These are all things IT can embrace and as a strategic vendor of compliance and security solutions to the enterprise, things we should and can help our customers with. Implementing least privilege across physical, virtual, and cloud-computing environments can also add to these savings.

Privilege Security Requirements

Banks, insurance companies, and other institutions are faced with the monumental task of managing authorization to mission-critical systems. These organizations have large numbers of internal and external users accessing an increasing number of applications, with each user requiring a different level of security and control requirements. In addition, these organizations must also address identity management concerns that arise from compliance issues related to such regulations as SOX, HIPAA, and PCI DSS.

High administrative costs due to account maintenance, password resets, inconsistent information, inflexible IT environments, silos due to mergers and acquisitions, and aging IT infrastructures make this even more challenging for organizations. Together, these factors are propelling the adoption of least privilege solutions across all industries. A least privilege architecture framework should consist of four continual stages running under a centralized automated platform: access to privileged resources; control of privileged resources; monitoring of actions taken on privileged resources; and remediation to revert changes made on privileged IT resources to a known good state:

- *Access:* Access includes the process of centrally provisioning role-based time-bound credentials for privileged access to IT assets in order to facilitate administrative tasks. The process also includes automation for approval of access requests and auditing of access logs.
- *Control:* Control includes the process of centrally managing role-based permissions for tasks that can be conducted by administrators once granted access to a privileged IT resource. The process also includes automation for approval of permission requests and auditing of administrative actions conducted on the system.
- *Monitor:* Monitor includes audit management of logging, recording, and overseeing user activities. This process also includes automated workflows for event and I/O log reviews and acknowledgements and centralized audit trails for streamlined audit support and heightened security awareness.
- *Remediation:* Remediation includes the process of refining previously assigned permissions for access and/or control to meet security or compliance objectives, and the capability to centrally roll back system configuration to a previous known acceptable state if required. Automation of the privileged access management lifecycle includes a central unifying policy platform coupled with an event review engine that provides control for and visibility into each stage of the lifecycle. See figure 9-2.

Figure 9-2. Risk Lifecycle.

Case Study: Using Least Privilege to Meet Compliance

DCI (www.datacenterinc.com), headquartered in Hutchinson, Kansas, is a premier developer of innovative core bank processing software and related technology serving hundreds of banks nationwide. DCI was founded by community bankers in 1963, and remains privately owned by several clients, with customers serving on their Board of Directors.

The corporation delivers technology solutions that allow banks to prosper and thrive. Because of the nature of the company and the services it provides, heavy IT support is necessary for the deletion, migration, and back-up of large amounts of sensitive data.

Dale Martinson, manager of systems and security at DCI, is responsible for managing the company's ever-increasing IT demands, including ongoing support for these procedures. To ensure the ability to support DCI's long-term strategic growth, Martinson and his staff performed a comprehensive evaluation of the IT infrastructure, including its safeguards and security functions.

The internal audit incorporated access-related areas such as reviewers, users' access rights, password rotation policies, and access history. The primary goals were to assess the situation and implement a solution that could be efficient and continue to comply with rigid financial industry regulations (such as SOX, PCI DSS, and GLBA).

"DCI is a very technical business, with many people requiring access to sensitive areas. Additionally, the majority of our 1,300+ users require multiple access rules and policies that impact our entire IT environment including, what specific areas can be accessed or when, during a specified time of day. Managing these policies manually was very time consuming and required cumbersome report consolidation. We agreed that we needed a solution to securely automate privileged access, reporting, and password management lifecycles across multi-platforms," said Martinson.

DCI selected a PIM solution following months of extensive review and analysis. The company sited regulatory compliance, ease of deployment, and scalability and flexibility of solution as the main purchase points. With this solution, DCI is able to:

- Automate the management of users/applications with authorized access to critical data
- Automatically purge unused user IDs and access rights from the system

- Generate reports to demonstrate compliance with a wide range of federal regulations

The Demand of Compliance Versus the Ease of Open Source

Ah, open source software! What better way for developers and administrators to reduce costs and speed the deployment of new functionality across the extended enterprise? If we are talking about least privilege, then we should revisit a subject bought up in Chapter 5 and that is Sudo.

What better way for IT admins to eliminate the proliferation of the root password throughout IT and development organizations? What better alternative to using root accounts to perform routine maintenance on UNIX and Linux systems? Just grant users the proper permissions in the local Sudoers files and you're in business. Oh, and the utility is free. What's not to love?

Now consider the compliance implications. Using Sudo for privilege management is like using a fish net to protect the fish in your pond from escaping. While it will catch most, there will always be holes big enough for something to escape.

As it turns out, deploying Sudo isn't as trouble-free as it may seem. Sure, Sudo is a far better practice than the rampant use of root, but that's not exactly the bar against which any security professional should be measuring internal IT processes.

One of the problems with Sudo is the ease with which it can be deployed haphazardly, without a lot of forethought, to address a particular day's privilege challenges. Mary needs to manage the office printers. John needs to reset passwords for people in the business unit he supports. Janice needs to perform server maintenance. The admin that restricts access to the root password without a ready alternative will become popular indeed, and not in a good way.

Enter Sudo as that ready alternative. Privileges can be granted quickly, independently, and with minimal effort. But before you know it, one privilege request processed on top of another leads to a hodgepodge of poorly maintained Sudoer files, all hosted on local servers with local log files and no audit trail to speak of. Better than the proliferation of the root password? Sure, but by how much?

Now consider more compliance implications. Many companies have standard compliance policies for Sudo, most of which require routine inspections of each Sudoer file to ensure that permissions granted to each user are appropriate. Not an easy task when the server count is in the hundreds or more. Many organizations find that a spot check of Sudoer files reveals permissions for users who have long since left the company—a guaranteed audit violation.

In reality, there is no substitute to carefully creating a privilege delegation strategy and designing a rollout plan that ensures security and compliance while minimizing the impact on users. While this can be done with Sudo just as it can with commercial tools, the fact is that commercial tools provide better guardrails around deployment and more sophisticated native features, such as encrypted logging and centralized policy stores, for enabling security protections and ease of maintenance. And the most robust ones provide an easy path to proving compliance, a challenge most administrators of Sudo deployments find all too formidable.

Walk on the Wild Side of a Failed Audit

We couldn't resist the homage to classic rock. Hopefully, you are familiar with the Lou Reed classic "Walk on the Wild Side" off of his 1972 *Transformer* album. If not, then check it out if you want a slice of New York in the late 1960s and early 1970s.

The reason we are using it as a metaphor in our chapter on compliance and security is because when we were talking with an IT auditor about compliance and failed audits in July 2011, this tune was playing in the background. Lou was singing "everybody had to pay and pay; a hustle here and a hustle there...hey babe, take a walk on the wild side" while we chatted about the right, wrong, and wild side of the dreaded audit.

- *The Right Side:* "You should have seen him go go go"—If you start by leveraging the resources available at SANS and ISACA, then you will be able to identify specific regulations pertinent to your audit requirements and what is necessary to ensure passing.
- *The Wrong Side:* "Everybody had to pay and pay"—Ignorance is not an effective defense of against a failed audit. Failed audits are becoming much more commonplace as technology facilitates better review of identity and access entitlements as well as user and administrator activities.
- *The Wild Side:* "A hustle here and a hustle there"—Now we enter the danger zone. Implementing partial solutions or still relying on

"trusted users/administrators" can deliver mixed results when the auditors do their thing. Decisions like using open source versus licensed software or if logging constitutes protection can have dramatic differences from one auditor to the next.

Ultimately, in a discussion on compliance and security, it is important to recognize that at the intersection point is the auditor. Most of your decisions regarding both security and compliance will be predicated to some degree on how you perceive your auditor will react and then consciously choose to be on the right, wrong, or wild side.

Case Study: Satisfying Auditing Challenges

The University of Texas MD Anderson Cancer Center was created by the Texas Legislature in 1941 as a world-leading institution for cancer treatment and care. In 2008 alone, nearly 1,000,000 people turned to MD Anderson for cancer care in the form of surgery, chemotherapy, radiation therapy, and immunotherapy. Four out of the past six years, MD Anderson has ranked the number one in cancer care in the "America's Best Hospitals" survey published by US News & World Report.

MD Anderson's world-famous cancer treatment facilities are backed by a powerful and secure UNIX network infrastructure that provides support to a faculty and staff of both MDs and PhDs numbering over 20,000. This network, which hosts in excess of 500 UNIX servers, houses confidential patient information and several critical financial and healthcare applications, all key to providing the level of service and expertise associated with MD Anderson.

With the HIPAA requirement deadlines quickly approaching, and critical patient care dependent on the reliability of network computer systems, the University of Texas MD Anderson Cancer Center, located in Houston, needed to find a secure way to manage and protect its IT infrastructure. Through a combination of inside systems expertise and outside software technology, security was able to not only meet current demands, but also prepare for future threats and requirements.

When David Nester came on board as the UNIX security architect at MD Anderson, he was charged with developing UNIX and web security for the institution's massive information network. Of particular importance for Nester were access control, authorization, root delegation, and auditing capabilities of the network. "The previous UNIX environment was not centralized, and it was difficult to understand what activities were being performed at each machine," says Nester. "I was assigned the challenge of placing controls back into the hands of our system administrators."

Nester knew that a strong IT infrastructure was vital to supporting the patient care services and overall mission of the institution. "The ability of our systems to operate effectively can substantially affect the critical medical care provided here at MD Anderson," says Nester. "If something were to go wrong, we would not have the luxury of time because people's lives are at stake."

MD Anderson selected a least privilege solution to sit on top of their UNIX servers and provide security and accountability by enabling systems administrators to delegate administrative privileges and authorization without disclosing the powerful root password. Other administrative tasks such as system programs mounting, performing backups, and adding new users can be delegated to individuals or groups at a granular level, thus reducing the risk of intentional or accidental damage. Additionally, it also grants granular user access to files, directories, and third-party applications and accounts (such as Oracle, SAP, and so forth).

Nester admits that he has noticed a significant correlation between the security enhancements provided by their server least privilege solution and return on investment in the form of system reliability. "[Our least privilege solution] allows us to tie the uptime of our environment directly to business productivity," says Nester.

In addition to granting delegated access across their network, it provided extensive auditing and logging features. This functionality provides a full audit trail of all actions occurring in important accounts such as root. Maintaining a complete audit trail of administrative actions now provides system administrators at MD Anderson with the ability to track exactly which actions have been undertaken by which users, when, and on which machines.

Nester was particularly impressed with the off-site logging capabilities of the solution as well. Prior to implementing the software, logging and auditing capabilities at MD Anderson were maintained on the individual machines for which the activity was being recorded. Nester says this was a significant security risk because it allowed hackers or internal users to manipulate records or erase evidence of system activity. "No other application allows you to have the audit replay ability like PowerBroker for Servers," says Nester. "Now I don't have to retrieve logs from each individual machine. The centralization is really powerful and cost effective."

Paralleling other healthcare institutions, MD Anderson is also faced with the daunting task of ensuring that all critical systems are HIPAA–compliant. Enacted by the US Congress in 1996, HIPAA establishes national standards intended to ensure privacy in electronic healthcare transactions. Security architects at MD Anderson have taken the opportunities provided by HIPAA to make sure their systems maintain all appropriate levels of security and privacy, while balancing security, productivity, and compliance.

Balancing Security, Productivity, and Compliance

If you regularly incorporate least privilege into your GRC discussions as you've seen in the MD Anderson case study, you will find that, when it comes time for the auditors to do their job, it will go much smoother than without.

As new security breaches continue to come to light almost daily, stricter compliance requirements are being put into place. Access control rules are being regulated and IT configurations are being mandated. The debate of security versus usability continues to be a hot topic, and the bottom line is always at the forefront of every decision. What can an enterprise do to be sure a costly audit won't derail the company? Follow these three steps to good IT health:

1. Start by eliminating administrator rights for all users who don't need them for tasks directly related to their job description thus removing the ability for inside data breaches (whether intentional, accidental, or indirect).

2. Have clear and separate duties for each user. With distinctive objectives about what each employee requires in order to do their respective jobs, the privileges allowed to each person will accurately correspond to the amount of privileges they need.

3. Don't immediately expect a "pass" on your first audit after implementing a least privilege solution. You cannot implement a least privilege policy and assume you're compliant. You need to continually audit privileges as work roles, new employees, and new data emerge and change.

Human nature once again is at play, so constant diligence is required across the extended enterprise. Implementing some form of identity and access management infrastructure isn't just a "nice to have." It's necessary. Once we accept this and make a place for it in our enterprises, the result will be a healthier, more secure, and more cost-effective IT environment

The Tradeoffs Between Security and Productivity

Since it's hard to analyze the tradeoffs between security and productivity, IT organizations can fall back on gut feel, rules of thumb, and past practices in making these decisions. The easiest answer is frequently to just follow the rules and regulations so you remain in compliance with industry regulations or current policies. As a result, compliance becomes a substitute for security. But are they really equal? Does being in compliance mean you have a secure IT environment?

We see a number of major challenges when staying In compliance is substituted for a well-thought-out IT security strategy. First, compliance-oriented policies tend to be backward–looking, making sure that past problems don't reoccur but do little to help anticipate new threats. Compliance also focuses on process rather than results, in many cases with a heavy emphasis on record keeping. And focusing on compliance can stifle innovation because new security techniques are needed to deal with new technical approaches.

Now don't get us wrong. Staying in compliance is a good thing to do. It's essential in many businesses. And the rigor that comes with staying in compliance is a necessary element of good security strategy. Maintaining SAS 70 Type II compliance, for example, lets everyone in the organization know that key processes are important and gives everyone an independent perspective of whether an organization is doing what they say they are going to do. And while it's often joked about, a compliance mandate often pays the bills for real security. If that's what it takes to upgrade key infrastructure, that's good too.

But it's clear that compliance doesn't equal good security. According to Jim Jaeger, director of DoD & Commercial Cyber Solutions for General Dynamics Advanced Information Systems, "virtually every breach we Investigate, that company has been certified as being compliant within the last year." And at its worst, Jaeger sees that "these compliance regimes give people an incredible false sense of security."

So while compliance is a great way set a minimum bar for security policies, you still need to take into account the real value of your data and the threats that face your industry and particular business. So we are back to having to do that difficult analysis on the real costs and benefits of security. And while there is no simple answer, there may be a different way to frame the problem. Can you implement security in a way that enhances productivity? Wouldn't that be great! The good news is that implementing a PIM solution can mitigate most of these trade-offs.

So, be wary of how proud your CEO can be with a bit of paper saying your company has met compliance requirements. As we've shown repeatedly in this chapter, the majority of data breaches were from companies who were compliant. Clearly the intersection of productivity, security, and compliance is a delicate balance that requires constant diligence, and of course that starts with the implementation of least privilege.

Weighing In

The balance between governance, compliance, and risk has always been a conversation that merits significant attention. In the world of IT security, all three of those are topics that must be addressed. Without one, the others will ultimately fail; therefore, appropriate time should be spent on the importance of each. The chapter outlined a lot of these, but let's hear opinions from our experts:

Secure Sam:

Governance is a crucial part of enterprise security. The rules and mandates must be decided on, and each of those must be enforced. This can be a very tricky thing—especially when geographical locations and political opinions get in the way. Particularly when it comes to least privilege, the concept of managing privileged access for people in different areas and with different perceptions of what they should be allowed to do can be complicated. Both from a logistical standpoint as well as from the stance that you don't want to completely upset all employees, there are definitely things to consider when governing least privilege in an organization's security plan. Being able to monitor and manage privileged identities, however, more than makes up for the challenges. The key is to follow the steps to good governance outlined—specifically the first one listed. It's vital to make changes in privileged access using a central policy change. Changing it centrally and then having it propagated and enforced across an extended enterprise solves the problem of geographic stipulations.

Least Privilege Lucy:

As the chapter pointed out, risk is a very subjective subject. The thing is, however, that certain behaviors and patterns always pose a threat and a risk to any given enterprise. For example, allowing all users access to sensitive data. This will always put your company at risk for a data breach. If the insider using his credentials to access said information doesn't manipulate or steal data, someone from the outside can easily hijack those credentials and take care of the crime instead. Therefore, to reduce the risk of such a catastrophic IT event, appropriate credential management is necessary. With changing job descriptions, new hires, and employees who either leave or are dismissed, functions change frequently. In order to mitigate these changes and avoid potential data travesties, managing privileges is crucial.

Compliance Carl:

I've said it before and I'll say it again—compliance isn't just about avoiding government fines. It's about protecting sensitive information and data within any given organization. Because different industries have different types of information and varying standards of security, there are multiple mandates that indicate how compliance is measured. Some of them, such as HIPAA, are based on protecting personal data with technical controls. Others, like PCI DSS, enhance payment security to help consumers avoid identity theft. The important thing to remember with these mandates is that they ultimately make your organization secure. The best way to do this is through a least privilege solution. Specifically, limiting access to sensitive IT resources while controlling and monitoring the use of data.

The Hard and Soft Cost of Apathy

"By far the most dangerous foe we have to fight is apathy—indifference from whatever cause, not from a lack of knowledge, but from careless-ness, from absorption in other pursuits, from a contempt bred of self satisfaction."

—William Osler, Founding Professor at Johns Hopkins Hospital

To understand the cost of apathy in relation to breaches and least privilege, we must first understand that how we manage risk impacts human behavior. If we box people in by removing all privileges, they will feel suffocated and likely rebel or withhold. If we give too many privileges, people will either feel scared of screwing up and breaking something, or take full advantage of their privileges and abuse the system. The key is to give them what they need, when they need it, and only then will they will feel safe enough to do their job well.

The primary theme of "good people can do bad things" cannot be overlooked here. Every example presented thus far in this book has magnified the unpredictable nature of human nature and its impact on your security, compliance, and productivity. The representative insider threats introduced in Chapter 2 as "Disgruntled Dave," "Accident Prone Annie," and "Identity Thief Irene" are right now sitting inside the perimeter of your extended enterprise. It's just a matter of time before apathy leads to them causing measureable harm.

So, why does the typical IT admin prefers to duck and cover when auditors or business executives come to gripe about why there are no controls on who can do what (auditors) or why everything is so locked down that work can't be done at all, let alone efficiently (business executives)?

> Q: Why did the ostrich stick his head in the sand?

> A: To avoid danger (actually lowering its head in high grass instead of self burial in sand).

Just avoiding the inevitable is never a good policy; you may as well just drop out, free your mind, and listen to Beatles records all day. For those admins looking to achieve the IT equivalent of Karmic Balance, then implementing a least privilege solution across desktops, servers, virtual, and cloud environments should be the next project on your to-do list. By implementing a least privilege solution, you will automatically facilitate the elevation (brokering) of admin privileges only when they are necessary in an auditable fashion that doesn't require handing out root or admin credentials.

If you keep up with current events, then you will find numerous examples of an over-privileged insider who misused their privilege to cost an organization millions of dollars—and reveal just how expensive your apathy can be/become.

Lessons from Jérôme Kerviel

A multi-billion dollar fraud from 2008 re-surfaced in the fall of 2010 in the news after a Paris court ordered Jérôme Kerviel, who engaged in over 1,000 fraudulent transactions, to pay a full $6.7 billion in restitution for his risky trades and serve three years in prison.

Forbes took their shot at what the events could teach us, which raised the compelling point that everyone is curious about—why is 100% of the blame being put on Jérôme? We don't know if the bank did indeed support Jérôme's risky trades, which were initially profitable. What we do know is that IT professionals have skills that are both useful and dangerous.

Kerviel came to the Societe Generale as a trader after being an IT worker at SocGen. *ComputerWorld* reports he used these skills to easily bypass the IT and process controls the bank put in place to detect fraudulent transactions.

We do think the single takeaway the news should remind us of are that the IT skills that are both dangerous and useful can be found anywhere. Protecting the enterprise from those with the motive and expertise isn't just a matter of mission-critical servers. The mindset that there will be those with access who have IT skills should be incorporated into security in everything we do.

Cyber Crime Can Be Lucrative

The economy of cyber crime is all too real—and too enticing. No longer sequestered to dark alleys and seedy bars, data thieves have almost unlimited options to market their ill-gotten wares to potential buyers. What this means to employers and organizations: the temptation to access and "appropriate" sensitive data may be too great for some to resist.

Q: So just how difficult is it for cyber criminals to sell data?

A: Shockingly easy.

Although the sale of stolen information often takes place completely underground in secret, closed to the public credit forums, people who want to join these groups can locate them quite easily. Once vetted by forum administrators to ensure they are not from law enforcement, they are invited into the network to market and distribute their wares.

And individuals need not even proactively seek out to divest an employer of sensitive, valuable data. Today, recruiters actively target individuals with local or specific data types—going so far as to even create job postings with criteria like "an established relationship with local banks" as a prerequisite for crime family consideration.

The ease with which individuals can locate black market buyers of data should scare every employer who provides mid- to low-level access to any type of sensitive information. Like some bizarro-world eBay, many of these markets actually have incentive packages. Competing prices, additional services, free trials, money-back guarantees, and terms and conditions are all offered. Prices for data are qualified like any other commodity: data is priced based on the domain, if the account belongs to a real person, and how popular it is. It can depend on the number of followers, how commercial the niche is, and if the data is real or bot-generated. Prices for online banking and payment systems depend on account verification.

To make matters worse, the cyber-crime black market, which has traditionally centered on distributing bank and credit-card details stolen from users around the world, has diversified its business model since 2010, and now sells a much broader range of hacked confidential information including bank credentials, logins, passwords, fake credit cards, and more.

So, while CSOs struggle to combat an ever-evolving crime organization that morphs and changes in a nanosecond, it may be the guy in the cube next to you that is seeking to supplement his bank account that could exact the most damage to your database.

How Much Is Your Code Worth?

In Chapter 2 we discussed the former Goldman Sachs programmer accused of stealing source code to take to a competitor for a much higher annual salary and $700,000 bonus. The ultimate question for you is at what point will your trusted employees do the same with your corporate information assets? When evaluating the cost of apathy you need to factor in the potential cost impact created when human nature defies legalities in favor of greed.

Lessons from Matt Miszewski

Arguably, former Microsoft employee Matt Miszewski is now a respondent in a recent motion filed against him for allegedly "retaining" some 600 MBs of sensitive and proprietary data. When he left the company to take up a position at Microsoft rival Salesforce.com, he was motivated by considerably less—at least as far as his personal return was concerned. Obviously, it's too early to pass judgment on such a case, or suggest that "retaining information" after leaving a company is just a posh way of saying stealing, but what we can do is comment on how Microsoft discovered Matt's supposed infraction.

Microsoft only discovered that the information had been taken as a result of due process in another, earlier case brought against Matt Miszewski. Mr. Miszewski had said he only took personal items with him when he left. Under discovery rules, the document cache stored on his laptop was produced. Simply put, this means that if they had not filed suit against Mr. Miszewski, they would have been unable to verify the "retention" of the data.

If we are to take 2011 Symantec/Ponemon Institute research seriously—which indicates that 59% of employees surveyed who lost or left a job in

2008 admitted to stealing confidential company information—then businesses should heed more attention to how they manage privileged access to sensitive data. Otherwise, they could be accused of aiding and abetting the theft by relying on trust alone. As our title suggests, he who holds the "over-privileged" ladder is as bad as a thief.

Whether via the desktop or from mission-critical servers, access to sensitive data needs to be managed on a needs-only basis. Employees get access based on the privileges they need to do their job, not how privileged (senior) they may be within the company.

One in 14 Can Cost You $129 Without Least Privilege

A May 2011 *PC World* article about malicious code and downloaded software reported "about one out of every 14 programs downloaded by Windows users turns out to be malicious." This didn't come from some random blogger or disgruntled day trader. It came from Microsoft's own research and, according to the article, "even though Microsoft has a feature in its Internet Explorer browser designed to steer users away from unknown and potentially untrustworthy software, about 5 percent of users ignore the warnings and download malicious Trojan horse programs anyway."

So the bottom line is that people can potentially take advantage of admin rights by downloading software and will have a 1 in 14 chance of infecting their computer with malicious code. According the Gartner, Inc.'s report, *The Cost of Removing Administrative Rights for the Wrong Users* (T. Cosgrove/April 2011), the primary difference between the two management profiles, "moderately managed" and "locked and well-managed," is user rights. The moderately managed profile assumes administrative rights are granted, while the locked and well-managed profile has them removed. The cost difference between the two profiles is $653 annually. Interestingly, 90% of the cost savings associated with the locked-down user is realized by the user, not IT. The user will spend less time fixing his or her system and doing other administrative tasks, because the PC is better managed.

Who's To Blame?

As we've waded through the hundreds of published insider breaches from just the last two years, what was a clear recurring theme was that of the vagaries of human nature. Not meaning to wax poetic, but it was always an individual who misused their own, or some other insider's, privileged access authorizations to IT systems to their own devices and/or gains. That begs two questions:

- What sets these people on their path to misuse of privilege?
- Are they personally responsible or is the organization's lack of controls partially responsible as well?

As we have pointed out many times—at the intersection of people, processes, and technology that make up the engine of modern business—it's human nature that is the weakest link. And, all too often, it's the tendency of almost the entire IT industry—vendors, analysts, and press—to ignore this.

Put another way, you can't rely on everyone being a saint or competent all of the time. It's not just malicious malcontents intent on destroying the system who can cause havoc, but also the negligent, misinformed, and downright nosey who can compromise sensitive data. In all cases, it's more often than not the case that such people have way too much privilege access—admin rights on the desktop, root password on the server—for the role they are required to play.

Indeed, when technology is to blame, it's not always the technology company's use; it's the failure to recognize the importance of technology, such as privileged identity management (PIM) systems, which can restrain over-privileged users without hampering productivity, which is at fault. With increasing costs arising from data breaches, including cleanup costs, as well as customer churn due to diminished trust, it makes sense not to rely on trust alone when it comes to employee and third-party access to sensitive data.

Hard Versus Soft Costs

All costs aren't completely as obvious as these examples would suggest. Simply stated, the principle of least privilege means that a user must run with the least amount of privilege for the least being performed. And what does this mean for you? It means you should look closely at eliminating administrator rights from users who don't absolutely need them, and elevate privileges for users who require them. Let's take a look at a couple of scenarios that will better paint this picture and its relevance to hard versus soft costs:

> *Scenario A:* A user in your company needs to install an application, and your IT department is slammed (as usual) and won't be able to help for several hours. Now that user can't install the application

necessary for their job function, which results in loss of work and overall production.

Scenario B: A user in your company is operating with full administrator rights, and is unfortunately a little too cavalier in their download habits. Because they are operating with admin rights, malware hijacks their computer and enters your database. Now your IT department has to get involved to fix and debug your system, which is both expensive and time-consuming.

Both situations color the importance of least privilege and further emphasize how important it is to find the right amount of privilege for all end users. Scenario A is of course the soft cost example, while Scenario B is the hard cost example. Both can have measureable negative impact to your organization if you are looking out for signs of these scenarios and implemented vehicles for accurate impact assessment.

The Soft Cost of Identity Breaches

Many of you have been a loyal customer of Wells Fargo for over a decade for lots of good reasons. But over the long President's Day weekend in February 2011, you may have received a call from them saying that one of the vendors you've paid recently has had a data breach and leaked your creditcard information.

They didn't tell you which vendor it was, but it was pretty easy to figure it out based on the fact that they verified every recent purchase up to the one you could determine it was.

This got us thinking about the "soft" costs of data breaches. Whether this breach was an insider or hacker, it must have cost a good chunk of cash to call thousands of customers and re-issue a card to each one.

Then, we wonder how/if Wells Fargo punished this particular vendor. For some companies, relationships—even more so than data—are the most valuable asset they have and data breaches can put a lot of different relationships at risk.

Case Study: Saving Help-Desk Costs

Care New England, located in Providence, Rhode Island, was founded in 1996 by Butler Hospital, Kent Hospital, and Women & Infants Hospital. Care New England is a not-for-profit healthcare system that offers a continuum of quality care, including two teaching hospitals affiliated with the Warren Alpert Medical School of Brown University, Butler and Women & Infants; a community hospital, Kent; a visiting nurse and home care/hospice agency, Care New England Home Health; and the Care New England Wellness Center. Care New England's strengths are based on complementary programs and distinctive competencies of their partner hospitals to its partner hospitals and agencies.

Keith Lee, End User Support Manager for Care New England, manages operations that provide end users with assistance for technical issues, which include desktop maintenance and administration. Keith's department supports over 4,800 desktops and over 10,000 desktop end users, including over 250 applications such as Horizon. Many of the desktops include laptops used by nurses in the field. The end users are dispersed all over the New England community in Massachusetts, Rhode Island, and Connecticut.

The large coverage area needed for support, along with the challenges of managing Horizon with all the other applications, created many challenges for Keith Lee's team. A substantial amount of help-desk calls were focused around the need to have administrative rights to install applications or run many applications that required such rights. At the time, the only solutions available were to either send an IT tech to perform installations in person, provide admin rights to users who need the privileged access to run applications, or give a user full administrative rights to perform installs or run applications.

"It took no time at all to realize that the options available at that time were unacceptable," said Keith. "Costs increased due to the rise in help-desk calls and tech hours needed to perform simple installs. There were also several security threats and compliance issues to Care New England."

Prior to installation, Keith's team spent a week building an automated process to test and migrate their policies into their selected least privilege solution. Initial deployment took only two weeks and Keith saw immediate benefits and the ability to operate transparently to the 10,000+ end users without pop-ups or consent dialogues.

Since the installation of a desktop least privilege solution, help-desk calls have decreased and users have the rights they need to safely install and run applications necessary to perform their job. The selected least privilege solution gives network administrators the ability to attach permission levels to Windows applications and processes with ease.

"I believe that if Care New England had decided to use another solution, we would have been forced to increase help-desk personnel, which would result in higher costs and substantial security concerns," said Keith.

Trust Alone Is Not an Option

At the RSA Conference in San Francisco in early 2011, we conducted a survey of over 111 IT professionals like you to find out if people trust their cloud vendors with their data. The findings were rather interesting:

- *71% of respondents wouldn't trust a cloud vendor with highly regulated data.* Some participants even scoffed at the idea and the few who marked "yes" emphasized their wish for a "depends" option. If we can't trust our cloud vendors, how can we get there? What needs to happen so we can put sensitive data in the cloud? Let's keep going.
- *60% of respondents don't know or aren't sure what their cloud vendors' privileged access policies are.* Cloud vendors need to provide this information to their clients, but they won't unless customers ask for it. This is where customers of cloud vendors need to be more proactive. Set requirements for privileged access, ask questions, demand reports, know their policies.
- *At least 24% of respondents estimate that over 50 administrators have privileged access to their cloud-hosted data and 55% have no idea how many IT admins have privileged access.* This is what makes privileged access from cloud vendors even more important—there's more IT staff and they don't work for your company. Is your cloud vendor doing what they can to limit the number of privileged access accounts with access to your particular data?
- *44% believe IT security has no influence or not enough influence in cloud vendor selections.* Cloud vendors are in a business and IT security costs erode their revenue and force them to charge more. If their clients don't see the value in security enough to make buying decisions based on it, that makes it a good business practice for cloud vendors to glaze over security best practices. The best time to investigate your cloud vendor's security reporting and practices is BEFORE you buy from them.
- *61% of respondents have over $100 million worth of data on cloud-hosted servers.* No surprise here. Your data is priceless. It's worth the security investment to protect it. One respondent said she wished there was an option for "priceless," because some data is worth so much, you just can't put a price on it.

- *36% of respondents have made some kind of efforts specifically for preventing a leak to WikiLeaks at their organization.* This is a bit off-topic from our cloud-centered survey, but it was interesting to see just how many organizations are really making an effort to prevent these emerging risks. Since WikiLeaks is primarily a risk only to very large organizations and is a reasonably new threat, the survey would indicate that the IT security industry has picked up on it very quickly.

In another survey that BeyondTrust conducted at the VMware show in San Francisco in the fall of 2010, over 55 respondents also had interesting things to say about trust in virtualized environments.

Has your company virtualized mission-critical servers?

> Most of them: 21 (37%)

> Some: 32 (56%)

> None: 4 (7%)

If one of your colleagues wanted to steal sensitive information from a mission-critical virtual server in the company, do you think they could?

> Yes: 28 (49%)

> Maybe: 14 (25%)

> No: 15 (26%)

What do you think your colleagues would be willing to do to get their hands on $20 million dollars?

> Kill someone: 10 (17%)

> Chop off their own arm: 9 (15%)

> Jump into a water tank with a shark: 10 (17%)

> Lose their job and leave the country: 20 (35%)

> Leak information to a competitor: 20 (35%)

> Wear a tutu: 23 (40%)

> Steal data: 12 (21%)

Bottom line observations from this survey include:

1. Sensitive servers are prevalent in a virtualized environment
2. Staff WOULD steal data for money and
3. Staff CAN steal data and the problem is incredibly clear

Calculating Your ROI for Least Privilege

So you've decided to implement a PIM solution because you've realized that a least privilege environment is a perfect way to eliminate the misuse of privilege from your corporation, help satisfy ever-changing governance mandates, and deliver on-demand entitlement reports and keystroke logs to auditors when required.

You've completed a comprehensive technical evaluation and gotten buy-in from all of the business stakeholders on cultural fit into the organization. Your final hurdle to overcome is a trip to the CFO to get a release on the budget required to procure and roll out across the enterprise. The only problem is that you know he is only going to respect your decision and approve the procurement if you can show a hard dollar savings and not just perceived soft productivity and compliance gains.

To quote *Hitchhikers Guide to the Galaxy*: "DON'T PANIC!" Many companies, large and small, have already implemented a least privilege solution across servers, desktops, virtualized, and cloud environments. Literally thousands of companies like yours have already taken the plunge, eliminated admin rights from their IT systems, and have realized significant hard-dollar savings across IT administration, help desk, audit, and governance areas.

Cost-Justifying Least Privilege

Ultimately, cost-justifying a least privilege solution, or any IT solution for that matter, is very specific to the way your company recognizes and monetizes specific hard and soft costs. We've given you many techniques and examples in this chapter that you can model for your individual needs, but remember to put values on:

- *Security:* Privileged access is critical for smooth ongoing administration of IT assets. At the same time, it exposes an organization to security risks, especially insider threats.
- *Compliance:* Privileged access to critical business systems, if not managed correctly, can introduce significant compliance risks. The ability to provide an audit trail across all stages of the least privilege solution is critical for compliance, and is often difficult to achieve in large, complex heterogeneous IT environments.
- *Reduced Complexity:* Effective least privilege solutions in large heterogeneous environments with multiple administrators, managers, and auditors can be an immensely challenging task.

- *Heterogeneous Coverage:* An effective least privilege solution supports across a broad range of platforms, including Windows, UNIX, Linux, AS/400, Active Directory, databases, firewalls, and routers/switches.

Weighing In

As you've seen, there is a cost that can be applied to apathy in relation to breaches and least privilege. By now, you should understand that managing risk can impact human behavior if done incorrectly. Those you set up as "under-privileged" will feel suffocated and likely rebel or withhold. Those who are "over-privileged" will either feel scared of screwing up and breaking something, or take full advantage of their privileges and abuse the system. Establishing a least privilege environment means the best of both worlds and creates the perfect balance. There are a lot of risks to letting insiders run free with mission-critical information. One of those risks is the cost it takes to mitigate a breach. It costs a lot of keep sensitive information secure, and least privilege is a way to keep those costs in check. Let's hear from our heroes:

Secure Sam:

It can be difficult to govern something that is constantly moving. An IT environment, as we've discussed in detail, is an ever-changing entity. People come and go, job descriptions change, and information filters in and out of the database. The thing that doesn't change, however, is the security that must accompany it. Another thing that doesn't change is the cost of keeping mission-critical data secure. Part of managing and governing a security plan, however, is identifying how to be secure AND cost-effective. Least privilege is the way to do that. By eliminating many of the reasons users need the help desk, the cost of keeping a company secure and compliant is an easy-to-fix problem. Least privilege truly mitigates the risk of admin-related tasks gone wrong, and as the person in charge of making sure all things IT run smoothly, it makes my job a lot easier.

Least Privilege Lucy:

Sometimes taking risks can be a good thing. Like building a financial portfolio or going whitewater rafting with friends. Risk in your company's IT environment, however, is never a good thing. Putting sensitive information into the hands of accident-prone or malicious insiders is a terrible idea. You cannot risk mission-critical information and put the security of your company in jeopardy. There are countless examples of organizations that have done this in the past year, and the results of their failure have been smeared all over the media. Because they took a risk and did not secure the inside perimeter of their enterprise, data was leaked and stolen. Information was made available to people with mal-intentions, and cyber criminals are growing all the more powerful. Because this is such a reality in the world today, organizations cannot risk allowing insiders the temptation to steal or manipulate sensitive information. That's where least privilege is an effective solution. By giving only those who need admin rights access to information, in addition to closely monitoring data and the use of it, companies can mitigate the significant risks associated with insiders and sensitive information.

Compliance Carl:

The idea of trust in an organization's IT environment kind of makes me laugh. Trust is a great thing, but not plausible whatsoever when talking about the security of mission-critical assets. It's amazing how many times trust is given when asked why certain users have advanced administrative rights. "They've been with the company for so long so I know they're trustworthy" or "I trust them—they would never do anything bad" are just a couple of responses I've heard many times. That fact is this: even trustworthy and well-seasoned employees can have their credential hijacked or make mistakes. Sometimes they have malicious intentions that no one is aware of. There is really no way to know; therefore, all employees in any given company should be treated the same, and in a way that ensures information is kept secure. Least privilege is the answer. In order to be completely compliant, users must only have access to the information they absolutely need. This is especially true in a cloud setting, as there are oft-uncontrolled variables at work. The bottom line is this: least privilege saves money, keeps information secure, and allows your corporation to remain compliant.

Final Thoughts for Least Privilege Best Practices

"Having a central view of all system administration reduces the costs of forensic investigation and allows for a faster response to security incidents while improving the company's ability to answer tough audit questions."

—Andras Cser, Forrester Research

You've invested in information technology and the associated infrastructure, applications, databases, and peripherals to assist your company in becoming competitive, ease administration, and satisfy reporting and compliance mandates. You've made decisions on physical servers and desktops.

You've decided on what to virtualize for cost saving and improved capacity planning. You may have moved some of that infrastructure to a public, private, or hybrid cloud infrastructure. You've hired an incredible team of employees and implemented IT security solutions to keep hostile outsiders from accessing your mission-critical systems. You've passed most, if not all, of your IT audits and have certificates to prove regulatory compliance. But, are you confident that you've avoided the potential of showing up in the next *Wall St Journal* article on insider breaches? Have you prevented good people, trusted employees, from doing bad things, intentionally, accidentally, or indirectly?

Intent Versus Action

Insider threats are a global phenomenon. Every company in every part of the world is subject to some level of insider threat. And guess what? Insider villains are just as unidentifiable in the UK as they are in the US. They appear just as innocuous in Poughkeepsie as they do in Perth.

If you have employees with excessive privileges or access to sensitive data, then they are at risk of intentionally, accidentally, or indirectly misusing that privilege and potentially stealing, deleting, or modifying the data. There is a very fine line between intent and action, especially when excessive privileges on IT resources are involved. We've observed three types of situations where intent and action may be in question:

1. *Intentional misuse of privilege:* In this circumstance, the over-privileged user has both intent and ultimate action to do harm.

   Remember "Disgruntled Dave" from Chapter 2? Now you know what to keep an eye out for and how implementing a least privilege solution can mitigate this dangerous inside threat.

2. *Accidental misuse of privilege:* In this circumstance, the over-privileged user has no intent to do harm, but their actions unfortunately result in measureable damage.

   Remember "Accident Prone Annie" from Chapter 2? Now you know what to keep an eye out for and how implementing a least privilege solution can mitigate this expensive inside threat.

3. *Indirect misuse of privilege:* In this circumstance, we find both intent and action at play with both an insider and a hostile outsider. The intent of the insider is to do no harm, but the action of harm is perpetrated on their behalf because their over-privileged credentials

were hijacked by a hostile outsider. The outsider had intent to do harm and the harmful action is perpetrated by hijacking an unknowing over-privileged insider.

Remember "Identity Thief Irene" from Chapter 2? Now you know what to keep an eye out for and how implementing a least privilege solution can mitigate this hidden inside threat.

We have reported on several cases already in this book where an insider has done everything from almost nuisance-level harm to the very heights of catastrophic theft in the hundreds of millions of dollars range. We will also analyze more as we delve deeper into the best practices observed. We travel frequently to visit resellers, customers, and prospects around the globe to discuss least privilege for specific business, geographic, and system level requirement (physical, virtual, cloud-based computing platforms). What always amazes us on these trips is the general belief that insider threats are solely a US-based issue and that employees are completely trustworthy everywhere else.

Nothing could be further from the truth. In January 2011, an article at computing.co.uk reported "ICO fines former Direct Assist employee for illegally obtaining NHS data." We're not sure if his action was matched to his intent, but clearly the results are the same.

Insider Threats Aren't Perpetrated By the Obvious

It would be nice if every villain inside your organization walked around wearing a big sign that broadcasts "bad guy looking to do bad things," but alas it is only in the cartoons and movies of Hollywood where you can always find the stereotypical bad guy: black top hat, curled black mustache, and sinister grin.

In real life enterprises, insiders look like you and me; just regular employees doing their job and collecting their paycheck. That's why "securing the perimeter within" is so important.

What are the boundaries within your extended enterprise (read: "the perimeter within")?

- *Physical:* This seems fairly obvious as the physical server and desktops throughout the organization; however, if you dig a little deeper, you discover a whole lot more. Mobile devices have infiltrated the enterprise as has supporting network devices that require individual privileged accounts to exist on the corporate network and a proliferation of databases and directories that also contain sensitive information. When defining the perimeter within, it is important to consider any- and everything that either has privileged account designations or can contain sensitive information.

- *Virtual:* Nowadays, a server or a desktop isn't always just a physical manifestation of a machine, but can be just one of multiple "virtual images" that exist on one physical machine in order to leverage the unused computing capacity within the enterprise. Don't forget to monitor the virtual sprawl that also proliferated because of this.

- *Cloud:* The *buzz word du jour* is cloud. Whether of the public (outsourced) or private (internally managed) variety, this is just making data and applications available via the Internet. Anyone who has been in enterprise computing for longer than three years will recognize this as better marketing for concepts that have been around for decades: SaaS/PaaS/IaaS for public cloud and portal/intranet/extranet for private cloud. Either way, this unique way of managing information also brings unique security, identity management, and regulatory compliance requirements to bear.

Now that you have a better understanding of what the perimeter within looks like, we can move on to talk about the types of things insiders can do to threaten your security, compliance, and governance policies.

Preventing Security Storms

How many times have you heard the old proverb "after the storm comes the calm?" And how many times have you just accepted "storms" as part of life? From our point of view, these downpours aren't actually necessary.

We also find, from an enterprise point of view, that the best kind of storm to steer clear of is the security storm. Do we have to wait for a rough and tumble tempest that completely derails everything we're working toward? Absolutely not—we can prevent the loss of secure information and keep our businesses calm and running smoothly, thus bypassing the storm and going straight for the calm. Let us show you how.

To prevent a "storm" in your company, take a good hard look at your enterprise. Is there a measure in place to secure your sensitive information from being blasted for the world to read? Are your users all operating at the superuser level? Are you setting yourself up for a problem, or have you taken the steps to bypass any damage? The reason for this internal assessment is clear:

all around us are unsettling reports of breached databases and purloined trade secrets. We're sure you've seen these intentional security storms: whether it's the Goldman code that was stolen, then sold, or the iTunes accounts that were hacked and up for sale..., both of these incidents point out how prevalent storms are in today's information security sector. But what is at the root of the problem? The answer is shocking. Many think its hackers, thieves, and malware vulnerabilities. While those can play a role, most breaches are caused by the abuse of admin rights.

Preventing security storms in your enterprise is easy. The answer is to take away the admin rights of all individuals who don't need them. Don't let them abuse their privileges; implement and practice a least privilege management solution. Give users access to information based on what is essential to their job. This will stabilize, secure, and streamline your system, thus preventing storms and allowing you to enjoy the calm.

Every organization has its own quirks. Sometimes leadership isn't involved enough for certain projects to be successful. Other times they're too involved. And sometimes it feels like everything is just too much of a mess. This is especially true when it comes to IT security and compliance across physical, virtual, and cloud environments.

It doesn't happen often, but when a CEO gets interested in IT security, often we're breathless. What do we tell her? What would the CEO ask about? *CIO Update* recently wrote on ten security questions your CEO should ask. So we wanted to put together the five questions you might be asked about administrative privileges and what your answers should be.

Q: Do you trust our staff?

A: Yes, of course! But we don't rely on trust alone.

Q: What processes are in place to protect these privileges?

A: Approvals, mitigated privileges, and keystroke monitoring.

Q: What are we doing to protect us from honest mistakes made by our own staff?

A: Oh dear, we do hope you can say that administrative privileges have been removed from desktop users!

Q: What are we doing to protect the cloud?

A: Enforced SLAs with our cloud vendors to follow the same policies we use internally.

Q: What's next?

A: Don't forget to plug the next project for which you need support and/or funding.

Bad Habits to Kick for IT Security

Isn't it amazing how easy it is to adopt bad habits? The crazy thing is that no one is immune; they plague each and every one of us. Whether we were taught incorrect practices or are just looking for shortcuts to make our lives/jobs/situations easier, each of us yields to poor patterns at some point in our lives.

It's when we allow these habits to interfere with the mechanisms keeping our enterprises safe that they become a huge problem. Maybe you think your actions won't matter because no one knows about them, or that your exploits won't affect the sensitive information within your company's database, or maybe it" just that you're not concerned enough to switch to correct principles. Whatever your reason for allowing bad habits to fester, it" time for a wake-up call! There's no room for these patterns in today's information security world. With cases like the Goldman Sachs debacle and the Vodafone incident showing how prevalent data leaks and cyber crime are becoming, it's time to shape up. But how can you take your bad habits and turn them into peace of mind? Start by kicking these four bad behaviors and you'll be well on your way:

1. Stop allowing your employees access to root. With this type of access, your people can access everything, including the privileges required to manipulate and share data.

2. Don't let desktop users run as administrators. When you allow your users to run as a local admin, you are opening your enterprise to serious security issues. You may think you're saving money by allowing this instead of multiple calls to the help desk, but in reality you're risking much more than money.

3. Stop bypassing logging. Without this system of checks and balances, you won't be able to granularly control what goes on in your company.

4. Don't assume that because you're using UAC, you're immune to data breaches. UAC is a great tool, but doesn't fully eliminate admin rights. It leaves gaping holes in your protection plan.

If you find yourself on the path to a security breach because you're choosing to maintain bad security habits, make the decision to change today. Kick these habits and introduce peace of mind into your security plan.

Balance Security and Productivity

Almost everyone has read the children's tale about the little girl who happened upon a house in the woods and went about discovering porridge that was too hot, too cold, and just right; chairs that were too big, too small, and just right; as well as beds that were too hard, too soft, and just right. It didn't end well when the bears came home to discover the intruder, but the lesson of extremes was forever implanted in your mind. Unfortunately, this lesson hasn't seemed to stick for most enterprises when it comes to security and compliance versus productivity and user friendliness (Figure 11-1).

Figure 11-1. Balanced security

When it comes to IT security, most organizations that we have interviewed fall into one of the two extreme camps of either:

- *Security Conscientious:* These organizations lock down every user under every circumstance. Specifically, they set up users without any admin rights and require a manager or help-desk technician whenever functions requiring privilege dictate. On the positive front, this strategy ensures compliance and to a large degree protects against harm, but may also impede productivity to significantly measureable levels.

- *Productivity Conscientious:* These organizations care more about productivity than they do security and tend to live by the "that can't happen to me" motto every time a new article shows up in the press for another organization's data loss. In this situation, users usually have full admin rights and trust is the only thing that protects from misuse of privilege and/or insider breaches. On the positive front, this strategy ensures very productive users, but the downside is the ever-looming threat of, not if, but when data loss will become a measurable impact.

Since you've continued to read this far into the book, we can only assume that you desire to achieve, or improve, your ability to satisfy both:

- *Balance Conscientious:* These organizations recognize the delicate balance of security to productivity as well as compliance to user friendliness and have moved to a least privilege environment. Establishing a centralized policy engine that can monitor and control privilege authorizations at a granular level can deliver the best of both previous extreme camps just described.

Delivering balance between security and compliance with productivity and ease of governance is a least privilege imperative. Setting privilege authorization based on set roles and policies facilitates an environment wherein fine-grained entitlements can mitigate the majority of privilege misuses discussed throughout this book. Let's take a look at how a specific organization found balance through least privilege.

Case Study: University Finds Balance

The University of Winchester, located in Winchester, UK, was established in 1840. The university combines their strong heritage with innovative learning and teaching to educate over 5,900 students in 17 different departments with over 650 staff members each year. The University of Winchester promotes the importance of intellectual freedom, social justice, diversity, spirituality, individual importance, and creativity.

Ian Short, Applications Infrastructure Manager for the University of Winchester, is part of the IT management team responsible for the operation of the IT environment across the university campus. The university predominantly runs a Microsoft site. All of the back-end servers run Windows Server 2003 and 2008 within an Active Directory domain. Ian's department also supports over 1,500 Windows desktops on campus (all running Windows XP) that includes over 7,000 user accounts. Many of these desktops include laptops used by remote employees in various locations. In addition, Ian and his team are responsible for 120+ applications, with a number of extra locally installed applications.

The challenge of managing user privileges in an environment full of students is complicated enough, but the dilemma only increases when you account for required applications. The team universally understood that they needed to eliminate administrator rights in order to decrease malware attacks and increase security. However, they also knew they couldn't lock down the entire network because of the 120+ applications they manage. Originally, the university used Admin Studio to deal with specific issues, but found this solution to be too time-consuming and unreliable.

"It became clear that in our environment something needed to be done," said Ian. "We were noticing a worrying growth in security risks and so managing user access became a priority."

Implementing a least privilege solution offers a simple, centralized approach, which reduces the threat posed by malware and elevates only necessary privileges. It satisfies all security protocols to restrict access to privileged users to a least privilege model.

"With this solution, we were able to lock down our users' access while still allowing applications to run where necessary," Ian explained. "It's the perfect solution for our IT needs. No longer are we required to 'punch holes' in our security in order to complete certain tasks."

With their least privilege solution, the University of Winchester has completely removed administrator rights among their users, while simultaneously providing adequate rights to perform the tasks that students and staff need. Some of the key uses include elevating privileges for 8 multimedia packages in their multimedia center, 24 applications on their desktops, and around half a dozen Windows functions. It also has significantly decreased the amount of time Ian and his team spend on support issues, which has significantly reduced cost, as well.

Passwords Authenticate for Least Privilege

Most of you already know that getting users to choose effective passwords is hard. This is particularly important to those of you looking to implement a least privilege solution that functions correctly, as you will need to accurately authenticate a user to know what access privileges to grant them.

While new technologies for user authentication are on the way, they aren't here just yet.

There are several options today for improving user passwords, but they all have issues. Requiring users to choose strong password often leads to them writing theirs down a yellow sticky pad so they can remember it. Password rotation is standard defense against password-cracking attacks, but a recent Microsoft study suggests password rotation just causes people to choose easier-to-remember phrases as passwords. Biometrics are expensive and far from foolproof. Two-factor authentication should be the norm, but is perceived as expensive and inconvenient. Even if implemented, it's still susceptible to social engineering and phishing attacks.

So there are no easy answers to ensure a user is who they say they are. As with all security decisions, you need to weigh the costs of a solution versus the risks, but practically we recommend three things:

1. Enforce strong passwords, but make it easier for people to create them. You can provide guidance about better ways to create strong but memorable passwords or suggest the use of passphrases rather than passwords. Finally, you could publish links to password strength testers like Microsoft's so people aren't surprised at the moment of truth when asked to input their new strong password.

2. For more secure situations, like systems administrators who may be able to access critical corporate systems, go with two-factor authentication; it's the current gold standard.

3. Finally, recognize that authentication will never be perfect. So implement least privilege at all levels to limit exposure. Not every user needs to be an admin on their desktop and not every system admin needs to access all systems with all commands

Implement Least Privilege Now Not Later

By now, you've seen the value of implementing a least privilege solution to establish boundaries instead of creating the proverbial security walls. This will facilitate not only a balance between security and productivity, but also assist with real-time governance changes across the ever-changing extended enterprise. Before we close the book, we'd like to offer a few key steps to success.

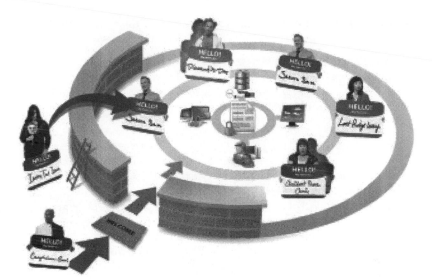

Figure 11-2. Least Privilege in the Enterprise.

Steps To Success

1. *Set Security as a Corporate Goal:* Enterprises may have trouble maintaining security because everyone is too busy trying to reach other goals. If you have problems maintaining security in your company, consider adding security as a goal for every level of management.

2. *Provide or Enlist in Training as Required:* For security to work, everyone needs to know the basic rules. Once they know the rules, it doesn't hurt to prompt them to follow those rules.

3. *Ensure All Managers Understand Security:* It is especially important that all members of management understand the risks associated with unsecured systems. Otherwise, management choices may unwittingly jeopardize the company's reputation, proprietary information, and financial results.

4. *Communicate to Management Clearly:* Too often, system administrators complain to their terminals instead of their supervisors. Other times, system administrators find that complaining to their supervisors is remarkably like complaining to their terminals.

   If you are a manager, make sure that your people have access to your time and attention. When security issues come up, it is important to pay attention. The first line of defense for your network is strong communication with the people behind your machines.

If you are a system administrator, try to ensure that talking to your immediate manager fixes the problems you see from potential or realized misuse of privileges. If it doesn't, you should be confident enough to reach higher in the management chain to alert for action.

5. *Delineate Cross-Organizational Security Support:* If your company has a security group and a system administration group, the organization needs to clearly define their roles and responsibilities. For example, are the system administrators responsible for configuring the systems? Is the security group responsible for reporting non-compliance? If no one is officially responsible, nothing will get done. And accountability for resulting problems will many times be shouldered by the non-offending party.

Weighing In

By now, you've figured out that we believe least privilege is a crucial component to IT environment security. Without it, over-privileged users can access (and abuse) sensitive resources and mission-critical information. Without it, under-privileged users can be so locked down that they are ineffective at doing their jobs without some level from the help-desk or management support to get past admin credential requirements. Protecting your data from insiders and their accidental, intentional, or indirect misuse of privileges is paramount to the success of your company's IT strategy. Let's hear what our experts think about that.

Secure Sam:

Governing an IT environment takes very granular attention to a lot of moving parts. It gets complicated, but having a well-defined plan mitigates most of the chaos that can come with sensitive data. As you know by now, least privilege is a necessity within that security plan. There are benefits that come from limiting access to mission-critical resources. We've talked about them throughout the book, but they're the driving reason that least privilege is in effect. To be able to centrally and efficiently manage a network of desktops, servers, and databases is paramount to the security of those devices. It's equally as important to prevent the risk of insiders destroying the delicate balance of a secured network, in addition to being compliant to federally mandated regulations regarding the protection of sensitive information. All these benefits are the result of least privilege, and are easily obtained by allowing employees access to only those resources they are entitled to based on their job descriptions.

Least Privilege Lucy:

As humans, it's very easy to fall into grooves. Some of these are good, and some of these are bad, but it's natural for us to create behavioral patterns. This is true in the IT world, as well; however, most of the habits formed tend to err on the side of bad. As an IT manager, it's a huge risk to allow people to run free among the resources I am responsible for. Even if people are the most trustworthy employees, accidents happen and inadvertent things come up. Privileges are misused, whether it's accidentally or intentionally, on a regular basis, and corporate security is too steep a price to be paid. Bad habits should not have a place in an IT environment, and least privilege is the way to counteract that. Users that don't need to run as administrators shouldn't, employees should never have access to the root password, and all activity should be closely monitored. The way to keep an enterprise secure is through least privilege.

Compliance Carl:

The best thing about compliance is this: by implementing it, most security infractions are mitigated. Earlier in the chapter, we discussed security storms. These can be prevented if compliance is a priority in your enterprise. If an organization takes the time to plan and execute a security plan that preemptively allows for the avoidance of breaches of secured data, that company is in a much better place as far as security tempests go. The best way to get compliant fast is to implement a least privilege solution. By now, you're aware of what that is. By now, you understand how crucial it is to the protection of your mission-critical information. Letting users have full access to data they don't necessarily need is both irresponsible and in direct violation of regulations provided to protect your enterprise's greatest asset. It's easier than it seems, and such a principle makes logical sense. Give users access to information based on what is essential to their job. This will stabilize, secure, and streamline your system, and make your enterprise a compliant environment.

Index